the common sense of flying

Your Guide to Stress-Free Travel

Boris Millan

Printed in the United States of America
Edited by Blue Note Editing & Writing.
Cover by Innovative Logos & Designs

Library of Congress Control Number: 2018911937
First Printing, 2018
ISBN 9-7817327675-0-8 (paperback)

BMP Media Group, LLC
Fort Lauderdale, FL 33312
www.bmpmediagroup.com

This book is dedicated to all of you who work in the Airline Industry, who day by day have to deal with good and bad travelers. Keep up the good work.

CONTENT

INTRODUCTION

Millions of people travel by airplane every day all over the world. Thousands of flights take off and land daily all over the planet. Some travel for business, some for leisure, and others for family emergencies. No matter your reason for getting on an airplane, I will show you how to make your experience as stress-free as possible. Just having a little common sense can make your travels more pleasant.

I have been called many names by passengers, including "Stuart", "Hey You", "Pssssst', "Stewardess", or just "Flight Attendant". I personally prefer the last one.

I have worked for a Major American carrier for many years, so I have seen it all, or so I thought. When it is least expected someone always tries to win the trophy for Worst Traveler of the Day. I also travel a lot for fun, so I certainly can see things from passengers' perspectives.

I truly believe passengers can control the amount of stress they experience when they travel. They can buy their tickets, travel, and arrive at their destination without having to file for divorce or end up in jail. Oh yeah - that last part is no joke; some passengers end up in jail, paying very high fines unnecessarily. I have logged enough hours in the air to be able to show you the right way to do it. Good planning is the key to a successful flight.

From booking until arrival at your final destination I will guide you - almost hold your hand, in fact - so your flight will be problem-free and enjoyable. No, I won't be your "Emotional Support Guide". Just follow my advice and you will have the best airplane ride you ever had.

CHAPTER 1

BOOKING YOUR FLIGHT

Booking your flight is easy. First you have to find out which carriers are actually flying that route. If you are traveling from Miami to New York there are many airlines that will be more than happy to take you. Many of you have already earned miles with your favorite airlines, so it is perfectly fine to use them for your travels. If the company you work for is paying for your ticket, then you may want to keep those miles for your next vacation to Europe or to a very nice Caribbean island.

Web search sites can be your best friend while booking. Search which airlines fly that route, then go directly to those airlines' web sites and book the tickets directly from them. Check to see which other airports are close by. Sometimes you can save money by traveling from another airport that is relatively close by, leaving you with more money to spend on your trip.

To dispel a myth, the majority of airlines, especially in the United States, will not give a discount to travel agencies or online travel sites. I see this all of the time in TV commercials. You may save some money when you buy a package that includes the hotel, flight, and car rental, but not if you only need to purchase the flight. Another reason I advise you to purchase your flight from your favorite airline is because, if you read the "small print" on those third-party sites, they are not responsible for any changes that may happen when you get to the airport, such as seat changes or even seat selection. Many airlines today have their own travel agencies and they can get you the same deal as those online sites.

If you are cost-conscious like I am, you will hunt for the cheapest ticket out there. Now, someone long ago said, "You get what you pay for", and I truly believe that.

Many airlines announce their deals on Monday evenings. On Tuesdays, therefore, all of the other airlines take part in what they call "Price Matching Adjustment". They want to compete, but this does not always work. There are many airlines that will not lower their prices, for the love of God. These airlines already have many loyal customers who will fly with them even if they are not the cheapest fare simply because of their great service, their mileage or the entertainment in the cabin. Those are all factors that can improve your flight experience. Unfortunately, some companies will only allow their employees to fly with one particular airline, so you may not have a choice if you are flying for business paid and your boss is paying for the ticket. Always remember to get those points or miles that you are earning, so you may use them later on to take a vacation with your spouse or your favorite cousin to Aruba.

One of the best ways to get the best deals out there, which is actually my favorite way, is to follow your favorite airline or airlines on social media. They will let you know as soon as they have sales available. Always try to sign up for their points or mileage program. Thousands of people travel each day without taking advantage of the many different programs most airlines offer, and mostly are completely free.

Keep in mind, when booking your flight, that many airlines will charge for bags, while others won't. Make sure you take that into consideration when choosing your airline.

Seat selection is also a very important fact to consider Many airlines will let you select your seat when booking directly with them. One of my favorite sites to visit before booking a specific flight is seatguru.com. You can actually search for a specific date and flight number and they will show you the type of aircraft it is, show you the seat numbers, describe which seats are good or bad, and give you a complete seat map of that aircraft.

My least favorite seats are the ones in front of the bulkhead or cabin divider. There are many rules about sitting in front of the bulkhead, but we will talk about those later. Also, many of those seats won't let you lift your arm rest. If you are tall like I am and you like stretching your legs, those seats are not for you, even though some airlines may charge you an extra fee to sit there.

My favorite seats when I travel in Economy are [drum roll, please] the emergency exit rows. I love those seats. They probably have the most leg room in the back of the airplane. Always check the aircraft type for that specific airline for a seat map and seat location and remember there are many government rules concerning the emergency seats depending on the aircraft flag or what country that airline is from. In the United States, FAA regulations state that passengers must be older than 15 years old and understand English to sit in those seats, so if you are traveling with your grandma who only speaks Spanish, those seats may not be for you. Regulations also prohibit passengers who use a wheelchair or cane from sitting in those seats, as well. A flight attendant will find you a better seat. Don't cheat; they will ask you personally on every flight if you are willing to help in case of an emergency.

In one of my flights to Bogota, Colombia, a lovely couple was seated in the emergency exit row and, as my job required it, I asked them in English if they were able to assist in case of an emergency. They smiled and looked at me if I were from another planet. Clearly, they had no clue what I had just said. Even though I spoke Spanish I had to ask them in English, as this was an American carrier. The lady said to me,

"NO ENGLISH".

In Spanish I told them they could not sit there, and that I had to move them to another seat. Suddenly, their smiling faces turned angry, and what I had thought was a lovely couple turned into the couple from hell. The woman called me every name in Spanish she could think of and refused to move. As I was the only Spanish speaker on that flight I had no option but to solve this problem myself. I explained the rules many times, but they would not listen to what I was saying. I even offered them a better seat up front, but they did not move. I had to make a decision. After talking to the Lead, we decided to call the authorities.

Thank God we were still at the gate; a company supervisor came, accompanied by a very large police officer. They were in shock. After we called the cops, suddenly they were not as loud as they were before. However, that was the point of no return for them; they were taken off the flight. For sure they were not going to Colombia that day, at least not with us!

Was it worth it for them to act like little kids when all we were doing was our job, even after we offered them a better deal? No; it definitely was not.

Unfortunately, there are other reasons passengers scream or behave badly during flights. For example, many people hate to fly. Every single movement of the airplane will make these people pray to every single deity there, and some even scream at their neighbors. This is not only embarrassing for them, but it is also very high maintenance for the cabin crew or passenger seated next to them. Try to get a seat near the exit rows at the middle of the cabin or up front; the airplane doesn't feel like it is moving as much when you are sitting up front. Buy the closest to the front of the airplane as your wallet can afford.

Many people decide not to select a seat with some airlines, however, thinking that they may get upgraded seats for free if the flight is full. (You know who you are.) Sometimes that works perfectly, but you could find yourself stuck in the middle of two big guys on your five-hour flight to Vegas. If the flight is full and you can afford the extra $30 to $50 for that aisle or window seat up front, just do it. It's not worth the risk.

Another very important subject you should discuss with your travel partners or family members is layover or connecting time between flights. You want to get there as soon as possible, right? Well, delays and cancellations do happen occasionally, so you should have a Plan B and give yourself time to go to your next gate when you arrive. Why rush? Because it's just not a good idea to book your tickets with less than an hour from the time you are supposed to arrive at your next departure.

Another common mistake is when people book a flight to go on a wonderful family cruise to the Caribbean that, by the way, leaves at 4:00 in the afternoon from Miami, but they booked their flight from Boston at noon. Seriously? They are just playing Russian Roulette with their trip. Planning a stay before your cruise should be part of your budget when preparing for your wonderful vacation. I highly recommend booking a hotel room near the cruise port at least one day before. Unless your job doesn't let you leave until midnight the night before, or if there is some other very important reason, there is just no excuse to not do this. If by any chance you have to travel the same day, buy the earliest flight so you can have plenty of time. Many cruise lines will let you come on board around noon, so you can start the party and spend more money on those delicious pool drinks.

CHAPTER 2

PREPARE FOR YOUR TRIP

Maybe you are like me; I love to pack for a two-day trip like I'm going on a month-long trip around the world. Hey, I have to have my shoes! Or maybe you like to travel very lightly, bringing just the stuff you need. If so, then you are my favorite passenger in the world.

Choosing the type of bag or rollaboard is very important. You have to find out first if your airline charges for bags and what their rules are regarding checked luggage and on-board luggage. There are some airlines that will charge you for the bags you bring to the cabin, as well. Finding this out before your trip will save you some money - as well as a headache.

You can also ask or do research to find out which type of aircraft is operating your flight. You can't bring the same rollaboard you can bring onto a Boeing 777 onto an Embraer 190 aircraft. Their available overhead bin space is different in size.

There are also rules by the Transportation Security Administration (TSA) that prohibit you from bringing certain items on a plane. For one thing, you can't bring more than 3.4 ounces of liquid through security, per item. There are exceptions to the rules, however, such as baby food, but I really recommend visiting the TSA's website for any updated information at www.TSA.gov. Also, all flights to the US from any country in the world have to adhere to those regulations, as well. Some countries are even stricter. If you are a family of two or more and you only want to check one bag, then put all liquids, including personal items like deodorants, shampoos, creams, lotions, toothpaste, perfume or colognes inside one bag only. This will be the bag that you will check at the ticket counter. You can also use the largest of all your bags in this case. Just remember the weight restriction for that airline; if your bag weighs 100 pounds, they will charge you a fee.

When I travel for leisure I like to bring my backpack. It is a large bag, but I only bring what I may need for that flight inside of that backpack; a tablet or laptop, headphones, a book to read, etc. If you are checking all your bags, especially those of you who are connecting, I recommend putting a pair of underwear and maybe another shirt, blouse, or t-shirt, just in case your airline decides to lose or "delay" your luggage and you have nothing to change into. It may happen; trust me. Also, do not pack that bag so heavily that you can't fit it under the seat in front of you or in the overhead bin. I can't tell you how many passengers I see every day with huge backpacks that can't fit anywhere. Just because you can fit everything inside your bag doesn't mean the bag will fit on the airplane. Almost all airlines will tell you what the largest measurements are for the bags you can bring on board or for the bags you want to check at the ticket counter.

We are all different and we may be traveling for different reasons, but make sure that you pack according to your needs. Think about how comfortable you want to be during your trip; especially for your trip to the airport.

CHAPTER 3

GOING TO THE AIRPORT

Once you have booked your flight, the next decision you and your travel partners will need to make is how to get to the airport. Even if you are flying by yourself, look at all the luggage you are bringing, including your purses, backpacks, etc., and don't forget to factor in the distance to the airport from home. Some airports in the US and around the globe are very easy to get to, while it can be a nightmare to get to others.

If you are driving to the airport, you must consider parking, as well. Many airports have plenty of parking very close to the terminals. Unfortunately, this does not apply to all airports, however. Also check parking prices; onsite parking at airports tends to be a little pricey: prices can vary from $10 – $60 a day to park. If you are going on a 10-day vacation, imagine spending $100 to $600 just for parking? I don't care how much money you have, that is just insane.

Many airports offer a shuttle service to the terminals from the parking garages, and if you have a lot of luggage, strollers, etc., it will be very inconvenient, not only for you and your family, but for others around you, as well. Just imagine a family of four getting into a bus full of people with seven bags and a stroller. That's not going to be pretty.

Now, do you remember when I said, "If you can't afford it, don't do it"? You have to take into consideration the costs for parking and traveling to the terminal as well as the time of the year you are traveling. Taking a vacation during the holidays is fun, but it also can be chaotic at the airport. Many airports prepare for this type of event or for special days by adding more parking on site or nearby, but that will just mean it will take you more time to get to your flight.

The best advice I can give you when going to the airport for a business trip or vacation is to give yourself plenty of time. When I am working or going on vacation, I like to get to the airport way before my flight departure time, to account for traffic, accidents on the road, time to find parking space, long lines at the airline counters, and going through security.

We were held up on a flight one time waiting for a customer to arrive, so we could close the doors and be on our way. Almost 10 minutes before departure time she was still nowhere to be found. All of the passengers inside the aircraft were growing impatient, and we all wanted to leave on time. Most airlines close the doors 15 minutes before departure time because they don't want bags traveling alone in case the owner doesn't show up at the gate on time, especially on an international flight. They will have to find and take that bag out, and sometimes it takes a little effort from the ground personnel to do that. If they have to do that right before departure time, it holds things up. Many flights are delayed for that reason.

Just before we decided to close the doors the passenger decided to show up. I could hear her stomping through the jet bridge like an elephant stampeding in Africa, screaming "STOP! STOP", very loudly. Now, if I am late for a flight and there are a hundred plus passengers waiting for me, the least I can do is apologize, thank them for waiting, and sit down. Not this woman! She communicated to me and all the people within earshot how awful the airline was and stated that she would never fly with us again. Yes, she was referring to the same airline that, just minutes before, decided to break the rules to wait for her a little longer. Before she headed to her seat, very angry and sweating like she just got off of an elliptical machine, she decided to tell me how horrible the traffic was. Just then I remembered something Ellen DeGeneres once said in one of her standup routines many years ago, which I often use in these cases. I pointed toward everyone else on the plane and asked,

"And how do you think everybody else got here? Did they helicopter in?"

If looks could kill, I'd have been struck by lightning right there. I took her boarding pass and guided her to the wonderful middle seat in the back of the cabin.

A second piece of advice I offer you is to take a taxi, Uber, Lyft, or even ask a friend or family member to take you, especially if you have a lot of luggage. It is just so much easier to get a ride. Getting dropped off right in front of your airline will save you both time and grief. If you are traveling for several days, it will even save you some money.

A while back, we used to share the airport shuttle to the terminals with regular passengers. It often seemed as though some people had left their common sense at home. We constantly had to deal with big strollers, huge bags, and annoying family members. It was a total mess. One couple with a baby had so many bags I thought they were moving permanently to Europe. It took them more than 15 minutes to get into the bus, even with the help of others. You can imagine why everyone else was getting furious. At least they were nice, though, and they apologized to everybody. Another passenger asked them if they were moving and they responded, “No. We are taking a short vacation to Turk & Caicos.” To me it looked like a very long stay in a very cold country, as though they had coats and jackets inside some of the bags, but why did they need so much luggage for three days on a beach?

If you don’t want to travel to the airport by car, many large cities have a train or subway that will take you to the airport, or at least nearby. If you are traveling light, it is the perfect way to and from your terminal. If you are thinking of traveling with a lot of luggage, however, please don't. It is just not a good idea. I dare you to bring four big bags, a stroller and a backpack onto a train in New York City at 4:30 PM!

Additionally, it is a very good idea to check in online. Many or most airlines will let you do so. This way, you do not have to leave your house four hours before your flight. If you are traveling internationally to or from the US, some airlines will not let you do it from home, however. Now, some airlines recommend being at the airport three hours before an international flight and two hours before a domestic flight, but this may change depending on the airport and time of the year.

The busiest travel days in the US are Thanksgiving and Memorial Day weekend. If you are traveling during those holidays, it will take you a little longer to get to your flight. I understand that you have paid more money to fly on those days but paying a little more for an Uber won't kill you.

My third piece of advice to you is to plan ahead. Check online with regard to the airport you are flying from or just ask your friends and family on social media. Either way, you should have a plan. Almost all airports in the US and many international airports have their own websites. You can see how convenient is for you to park there, get directions, and even check to see if there is space available for your car if you decide to drive yourself. Also, make sure you know where you are going. Far too many people arrive at an airport with no clue where they are going. They are totally clueless. You won't have a problem at small airports like Long Beach, California, but if you are traveling from airports like JFK International, Hartfield – Jackson in Atlanta, Dubai International, Madrid – Barajas, or even from Fort Lauderdale in Florida, you will save time knowing where your airline is located.

CHAPTER 4

AT THE AIRPORT

When I'm at the airport, it always surprises me to see people wandering around looking like their alien spaceship just dropped them off outside and they have no idea what an airport is. I'm not judging. After all, maybe this is their first time in an airport and they are as surprised as I was when I was a kid and went to the airport for the first time. Often, people are awestruck just by the look of the airport. There are airports so beautiful that you can't believe your eyes. Some are very modern and spacious, while others are very classy and full of beautiful architecture. Many cities have spent millions of dollars updating their airports, so passengers may feel comfortable and amazed by their beauty. While waiting for my flight to Dubai at Singapore Changi Airport I noticed a piece of hanging art that was just beautiful. I was amazed by the way it constantly changed shape, and it was soothing to watch. I will always remember how relaxed I felt, like I was at a beautiful gallery, rather than at an airport. The spell was only broken when I had to go and check in with my airline.

If you aren't sure where you are going, just remember: one thing almost all airports have in common is good signage. There are signs everywhere telling you where to go and where you are. Before you stop a random stranger to ask where your airline's ticket counter is, just look up. It may be right in front of you.

Asking for help is not a problem; we all need a little help from time to time, but common sense should be employed, too. Now, I think I am a very nice guy, and I swear to you I really love my job. However, one of my pet peeves is when someone with no common sense comes to me with a very stupid question at the wrong place at the wrong time. A while ago I decided to park across from the terminal where flight was leaving from that day. I was in a rush and, as I was crossing the small street that divides the parking area from the terminal entrance, I saw a woman get out of her taxi, looking at me as I crossed the street. I am not that bad to look at, so I thought she found me handsome or that she was attracted to men in uniform. Just as my ego hit the roof, she stopped me and asked,

"Excuse me, do you know what gate Philadelphia is?"

My ego deflated faster than a burst balloon. For a second, I thought it was a joke, but she was *not* joking. I stopped, closed my eyes, put each index finger on my head and responded to her by moving my head very lightly and saying, "Mmmmmm…. It's not coming to me... mmmm...you are going to go inside and look at one of the many tv monitors we have inside". I opened my eyes, and she was starting at me, totally stunned. I understand. It was very sarcastic of me to give her that answer, but she had it coming. I actually felt bad, so I guided her inside to her airline.

Almost all airports have very clear signs that show where each airline is located. Just follow the signs. Many airlines spend millions to make your check-in process a little easier. One very useful tool airlines have now are the kiosks located right up front, which I really love. Sometimes you can even print your luggage tags yourself. These kiosks are very passenger-friendly.

If you are not technology-friendly, however, and you get nervous just looking at a computer screen, you can seek help from an actual human being. Almost all airlines have someone standing by to help you check in at the kiosk and guide you step-by-step all the way. You may get lucky; you may find yourself being helped by that special person who loves his or her job so much that they smile constantly while teaching you where the letters on the keyboard, so you can enter your very difficult last name. They may be so nice and so patient with you that you may want to keep them with you all the way to your final destination and hold their hands through security and to your gate. No, unfortunately you can't do that.

Some of you may not be so lucky. You may get that horrible person that hates their job and cannot wait for their shift to be over to go home. Do not take it personally, though. They may be miserable at home, as well, and they may treat their own family the same way. All you need is for them to show you how to use that kiosk. After that, you may not ever see them again. If their treatment was really beyond awful, you can contact the airline and let them know. Always remember, however, that we are not perfect, and that person may be dealing with their own problems. Still, though; there is no excuse for not doing their job.

Now, remember; kindness and politeness always pay off. If by any chance you have to go to the airline desk, either to give them your checked luggage, to check in, or just to ask a question, there are three magic phrases that may get you very far when you travel: *GOOD MORNING, GOOD AFTERNOON,* and *GOOD EVENING.* Just being nice can help you get that upgrade you were looking for or that better seat in Economy you were not expecting. Smiling helps, too. A smile and a dose of genteel behavior can make your trip a little more pleasurable. Don't expect to get upgraded every time you are nice, though, although it does help. If you do receive an upgrade, always remember to say *THANK YOU.*

Okay, now that you have navigated your way through the big, scary mothership known as the airport, and you've made it to the counter. The next step is checking your luggage. If your airline offers free checked luggage, I suggest you take advantage of it. Why carry luggage when you are flying if they are willing to make your life easier? Many business passengers don't do so because of time constraints; perhaps they have a meeting they need to get to quickly. Also, they probably won't be carrying a bag weighing 100lbs.

If you are traveling with your family, especially with children, I really recommend taking advantage of the airline's offer for free checked luggage. I also recommend checking all your luggage when you are traveling with family if there is a fee. If you decide to bring your bag to the airplane, please do not expect others to help you carry your bag. It is not a flight attendant's job to put your heavy bag in the overhead bins. Flight attendants are there for your safety and to make sure you have a pleasant flight. You have a choice; you can make it simple or complicated. It is totally up to you.

You and your family will be glad you checked your bags when you travel to certain airports that don't use jet bridges to connect to the terminal. This applies especially to small airports in the Caribbean and all around the world, such as Cartagena in Colombia, Punta Cana in the Dominican Republic, Barbados, Kona in Hawaii, and many others, even including some regional airlines. At these airports, you have to use stairs and walk all the way, and that is simply not fun to do when you have to struggle with bags.

As I mentioned before, give yourself plenty of time to go through airport security. Security is not taken lightly, especially after 9-11, not only in the US but all around the world. I would have thought people knew the rules by now, but nope. I see TSA agents taking things from passengers every day, from knives to bottles of water. Remember the website I mentioned earlier, TSA.GOV? Please visit it. After all, there are rules we all have to obey, even crew members like me. If you know you can't bring water, don't bring it. Why spent $5 on a bottle of water they will probably take from you at security? Don't get upset if they take the big 8oz bottle of special shampoo for your hair, the bottle of vodka you were trying to hide in your purse, or that big knife you use at home to peel your apples. Nothing will change if you get angry or start screaming at the TSA agents. They are federal workers following rules and they also deserve respect from you. I know some of them are not as pleasant or friendly as you may like, but they are just doing what they are supposed to do. Don't ruin your trip because of that.

With regard to X-rays, always let TSA agents know if you have any medical condition that will not permit you to be x-rayed. If you are in doubt, always ask first. It is your right to do so.

Travel with as little metal as possible. Anything can set off the alarm and they can make you go back or even send you for a secondary screening, which you may find a little uncomfortable. Make it easy for yourself. As you approach the x-ray machine, have everything ready; your belt, watch, cellphone, shoes, laptop, or anything else that could trigger the scanner. The more stuff you bring with you, the longer it will take to pass the checkpoint. They may also ask you to take your jacket or sweater off. If you forgot to take your bottle of water out of your bag, you won't go to jail for that. They will just keep it. If you forget to take your gun out of your bag before putting it in the X-ray machine, then you may have to visit the county jail for a night. You can make it as easy or hard as you like. Before you enter the security line, make sure you have your boarding pass, either paper or electronic, along with a government-issued identification. Your library card won't work.

Always remember to eat before coming to the airport. Some people can't eat breakfast in the mornings or they get nervous before their flight, so they don't eat anything at home. If that is the case, you can prepare something at home and bring it to the airport - even something as simple as a sandwich, - and take it on the plane with you. Remember, it is only liquids over 3.4 oz that are not allowed; nobody said anything about forbidding bread or ham.

If you are on a special diet for health or religious reasons, do not expect the airport to have exactly what you eat at home. For those of you who travel on a budget, always remember, airports are expensive. That guava and cheese pastelito you bought the other day at 7-Eleven for 65 cents would cost you almost $5 at many airports. Restaurants inside the terminals will charge you an arm and a leg for your food, except for a few chain restaurants at some airports that will not change their regular prices. On a budget, paying over $11 for a salad that you may or may not like is a lot of money, especially if you have a big family. Think about it; you already spent over a hundred dollars and you are not even starting your vacation yet. Do you want to blow your budget on airport food?

Of course, if you are traveling on business with that wonderful, magical corporate American Express, I'm sure you are very careful with your company expenses, right? Or maybe not… In that case, you can totally disregard everything I said about buying food on a budget at the airport. You can buy that $15 quesadilla that will make you question what was inside of it long after you've eaten it, or you can buy that $14 fruit platter that comes with five grapes and four pieces of plastic cheese that you will regret later on.

The majority of large international airports have a good selection of items for you to eat and drink. Many local airports offer local cuisine for you to enjoy. Miami Airport in Florida is the perfect example. Wherever you go in any terminal inside the beautiful and tremendous MIA you are going to find many Latin restaurants serving similar food, but with their own chef's touch. Even at sushi restaurants you may find delicious fried plantain with mango sushi that the Japanese had no idea existed.

You also may find alcohol served almost everywhere. There are bars everywhere, of course, depending on which airport you are leaving from. Even at small airports you may find a bar. Alcoholic drinks at airports may be a little more expensive than usual and not as strong as the drinks you'll get from your local bar, though; after all, they don't want you to get drunk before your flight. Now, keep in mind that everybody reacts differently to alcohol. I can have many drinks before getting drunk or appearing intoxicated, but you may be different. Most airlines in the USA and throughout the world will not let you board an airplane if you are drunk, so keep an eye on how much you're drinking. Some bars may actually tell your airline to keep an eye on you if you are starting to behave strangely. They do not want to be responsible.

If you love beer and you feel you must have one before your flight, be sure to finish it at the bar. You are NOT allowed to bring any open alcohol container inside an airplane or near a gate. If you are seen with a beer or any alcoholic beverage in your hands before your flight, you will be asked to get rid of it or they may even stop you from getting onto the airplane if they think you are intoxicated. That is the law. If an airport agent or crew member asks you to put it in the trash, don't say a word; just do it. If you open your mouth even just apologize, and they smell whiskey on your breath from afar, you may not be going anywhere soon. Be smart and do not try to prove anything. This is neither the time nor the place.

Along with some of the minor inconveniences I have mentioned, airports can also offer some conveniences and amenities. Now, some airports are nicer than others; they are more comfortable and offer more amenities, yet you'd be surprised how many important airports still have no place to charge your phone, tablet or laptop. Therefore, you should come prepared by charging your devices at home before you leave. I constantly see people sitting on the floor throughout the airport trying to charge their phones. First of all, the floor is disgusting. Imagine all the people who walk all over that floor every day with their dirty shoes. Why do that when many airport restaurants may do you a favor and charge it for you while you are eating or at the bar, and when many seats at some airports may have electric plugs ready for you? I see more and more charging stations at many airports now. They are very conveniently located throughout all of the terminals for anyone to use, but there are also rules that apply when using these stations:

- If you get there first, you charge first. Easy as that.
- Do not leave your phone alone. If you leave your phone alone while charging you are very naive and trusting. There may be no phone when you come back.
- If you are not charging anything, do not sit there. Leave the seat for others who may need to charge their phone.
- There is a time limit to charge your phone. Some say that you should limit yourself to 60 minutes, especially if the terminal is full and others are waiting.
- Do not place drinks on top of devices. If you spill the drink and get other people's devices wet, that may get you in trouble, especially if it is an expensive laptop.
- Do not place your luggage or any bag on top. Put it under the seat.
- Do not plug five phones at the same time, unless of course the place is empty, and you are the only one there.

- Keep your children away from the charging stations. As much as you love your kids, they are yours and yours alone.
- Do not ever look at others' devices. Don't be rude. It is not your business to look at what others are doing on their laptops or cellphones.

You would be surprised by how many people do not have the common courtesy of refraining from doing anything I just mentioned.

While you are at the terminal, whether sitting at the bar enjoying your beer, charging your phone, or even just waiting for your flight, do not leave your luggage alone at any time. There are very serious airport and security measures in place for everyone's safety. If you go to the bathroom and leave your bag at the gate, it may be gone when you come back. They don't care how much screaming or begging you do when you return and find that your bag is gone. Keep it with you at all times. It's for your own protection, too. You don't want anybody to put something "funny" inside your bag and use you to transport their fabulous merchandise inside your bag. You don't want any surprises later on.

You also cannot bring your lovely pet Lulu and let her walk all around the terminal with you. Unless Lulu is a service dog, the majority of airports in the US and in other countries will not let you take Lulu for a walk around the gates. You may be fined by airport personnel or the local police if you do, so keep Lulu inside the carrier at all times. For your convenience, many airports are "pet friendly" and will have a place for Lulu to do number one or two.

If Lulu is your "emotional support pet", make sure all required documentation is up to date. Not all airlines consider emotional support animals to be service animals, so they may not let you fly unless you pay the fee. Other airlines do not allow *any* pets in the cabin, so make sure you check with your airline before you bring lovely Lulu to the airport.

As I mentioned before, airports worldwide spend a pretty penny, so you will be comfortable and to take away the stress of flying. Why not take advantage of whatever conveniences they offer?

CHAPTER 5

BEFORE YOUR FLIGHT

One of the most important phases of flying is boarding time. Countless people miss their flights every day for really stupid reasons. Unfortunately, too many people make this one of the most difficult parts of flying, when it should be one of the easiest.

You need to be at the right gate at the right time. Many airlines will start boarding their flights from thirty minutes to one hour before their departure time. Of course, this may vary depending on the type of aircraft or airline. If the boarding time is not listed on the information monitor at the gate you can always ask an agent if you have any questions regarding boarding times. If the agents are busy and you are already at the gate, just wait for announcements from the airline representative.

Boarding can be a simple task if you let it be. All you need to do is look at your number or group and wait. If they are not calling you, why are you blocking everyone else who is actually listening and paying attention?

I can't stress enough how important it is to pay attention to all announcements and gate change information. The first thing you should do when you get to the airport is to check your gate number.

Airlines change gates at all times due to weather, aircraft availability or for any other reason they may have. This happens all the time, at all airports and with all airlines. Don't get upset if your airline changes its gate to another; there is a reason for the change. Things happen even to the best of airlines.

Like many passengers, you can check in online, sometimes the day before, and bring your tickets printed on a piece of paper, and always check your gate information when you get to the airport. In fact, before boarding time you should always double check that you are at the correct gate for your flight. This may be obvious to you, but thousands of people miss their flight because they didn't double check.

Once I was working a flight and I arrived at the gate a little earlier than usual, so I decided to sit next to my gate while they started boarding a flight to Newark, New Jersey. Next to me was a young guy listening to music while texting or writing something on his phone. I certainly *hope* he was listening to music, because he was dancing at the same time he was typing. Anyway, the flight was almost boarded, and the agent called several names on the loudspeaker. Agents will generally call passengers who are checked in for the flight but not at the boarding gate. She kept calling and calling a couple of names several times, and loudly. She finally decided to close the flight as well as the entrance door to the jet bridge. I even saw the flight pulling off the gate. A little later my airplane arrived, and I went to the gate to get my paperwork. Suddenly I saw the same guy who had been dancing and texting asking the agent what time his flight to Newark was boarding. We looked at each other in surprise. After the agent informed him that his flight was gone he became extremely angry. Everyone around could hear him screaming; that's how angry he was. The agent remained patient as she informed him that they had called his name several times, but he never responded. I remember seeing him sitting in front of the gate, listening to music and texting while they were boarding his flight, but I decided to say nothing and leave that to the professionals. He calmed down after a bit and was told to go to an information desk to have his flight changed to the next one.

Unfortunately, this happens more often than you think. You can get distracted by anything, but you have to stay focused and be alert for any changes that may happen.

Even weather can alter your travel plans. If the weather is horrible and there have been many delays and cancellations, be aware that your flight may change, too. Keep an eye on those tv monitors in the terminal. In addition, many airlines - especially major carriers - have applications you can download from your phone or tablet. If you use the app and something changes you will be the first to know; often before the agents at the gate know.

Another day, while waiting for my flight, a lovely couple missed their connecting flight to the Caribbean because they didn't check the monitors at the terminal. They had printed their boarding passes the day before in California, and when they arrived they went to the gate shown on their boarding passes. Even though their flight information was not at the gate they were waiting at, they never took the time to ask an agent or even to check the monitors around the terminal. I felt very badly for them, but it was completely their responsibility to check for their flight. According to the agent, their names were called several times before the doors were closed. They were put on the next flight, but they had to spend a little more time at the airport than they'd planned.

Remember; no airline in the world will wait for you unless you are coming in on a delayed connecting flight and they decide to do so. This is totally up to them, depending on the circumstances and how many connecting passengers are on the flight. It is your responsibility to make sure you are at the right gate at the right time. Screaming, insulting or banging on airport property is just going to get you arrested. It is just not worth it. A commercial airline does not have to wait for you. If you are not at the gate, you won't fly. As bad as it sounds, it really is that simple. Stop blaming others, especially airline employees, for your mistakes or for any personal problem you may had before you came to the airport that may have caused you to be late. If the flight leaves without you and you know it was totally your fault, relax, go to the gate and explain the situation in a very calm manner. Nothing will change at that point with regard to your flight leaving without you, but you can ask the agent very politely what you can do to make it to your destination. Airlines can put you on the next flight free of charge if they like. Being polite can help you greatly in these situations.

I was working a flight recently to Mexico City. It was "one of those days": the weather was horrible all over the country. There is nothing we can do when Mother Nature decides to bless us with terrible weather. From the moment I was driving to the airport and I saw those black clouds, I knew it was going to be a very long day. Flights from every airline were coming and leaving very late, and some airplanes were even landing at nearby airports due to the storm. We had to change gates twice; thankfully, still in the same area. Our airplane was coming from New York and it was more than three hours delayed. Passengers were not very happy, but they were also understanding of the situation. A couple of gates away, there it was; a beautiful Airbus, just like the one we were supposed to take. That flight was scheduled for later in the afternoon. All of us working the flight looked at each other and asked the Captain if he could do something. After a few phone calls, our operation department gave us the green light to take that airplane. Thank you, Lord, as we were not getting paid for any of that time we spent waiting for the original airplane. We decided to take the other aircraft, thinking passengers would be as happy as we were. After all, there would be no waiting four hours for our flight. However, when the agent broke the news to them on the speaker phone and told them we had to change gates again, from gate 10 to gate 7, all hell broke loose. The passengers got very upset. As we were already walking to our new gate, just a few meters away, we could hear people talking and cursing so loudly in English and Spanish that for a moment I thought no one was going anywhere any time soon. Yet all that time we were thinking we were doing the right thing. You never know.

Airline workers at the gates, or *agents* as we call them, are very busy right before each flight. They need to handle many things that go with working a flight, such as making sure all passengers are checked in, determining how many bags they have, collecting personal information required to travel, passports, etc. They are also busy answering valid questions that many passengers have. Asking every five minutes when the flight is boarding is not going to change anything; not even the boarding time. If you see on the gate monitor that the flight is delayed, it is because it is delayed. Usually the agents will explain the reason for the delay and give you an estimated time for departure. You have no idea how many people will come to the gate to ask the same thing the agent just told announced. Sometimes after three or four people have asked the same questions, agents will use the loudspeaker or P.A. system to give the same information again. Yet people STILL come to the gate and ask exactly the same thing, over and over again.

When boarding time finally arrives, airlines board in different ways. Some airlines do it by seat numbers, and others by group numbers or letters. Familiarize yourself with your boarding pass. Agents will explain the process right before boarding, so please pay attention so you do it correctly. If you are traveling on an airline that has assigned seats, there is no need to stand in line at the gate thirty minutes before the flight. I see this trend more and more as I travel through different airports. Keep the gates clear. You won't win an award for standing at the gate, so you might as well sit and wait. First, they will call for disabled passengers and people who take a little longer to board an airplane. This includes passengers in wheelchairs. Unfortunately, many people who do not need a wheelchair ask for them for this same reason. Boarding first: my Aunt on my mother's side is an expert in doing that. Some flights have up to twenty wheelchairs when they board and only five when they get to their final destination. We call them MIRACLE FLIGHTS. Some passengers are suddenly cured on the trajectory to their final destination. Very interesting indeed. Unfortunately, there is nothing we can do when customers request wheelchairs; we have no way of proving whether they really need them.

After disabled passengers board, they will probably board first class passengers or customers with loyalty points or miles. The higher your status, the higher your boarding priority. These passengers travel a lot, so they deserve to board first. Usually people who travel that much know all the rules and tricks to an easy boarding and flight. These are the passengers who will be the easiest to assist or serve inside the aircraft. Many business people just want to work on their laptops and be left alone. There are others, especially those who just attained their status, who will make sure they get their money's worth. One of the reasons airlines give passengers priority to board is so they can find overhead bin space before other passengers arrive. After all, overhead bin space is shared among everybody. If you have Platinum or Gold status and you missed the priority boarding and waited until the end to bring your big suitcase and computer bag, then guess what? It is a full flight with no more space. Do not by any means take anybody's luggage down to put yours in the bin. You had your chance. Crew members will try to accommodate you as much as they can, maybe offering another space away from your seat. This is when many Gold or Platinum members become like little kids and throw tantrums in front of everyone else. How embarrassing is it for a grown man or woman to act this way, just because it did not go their way? Again, asking politely and respectfully can get you far. We may even let you use one of our compartments to place your bag. All you have to do is be nice.

Next, they will start calling by groups or numbers, depending on the airline. If they have not called your group or number yet, do not try to board; just wait your turn. They will know and send you back in line. Would that be embarrassing enough for you?

Many airlines, especially on full flights, will offer to check your bags at the gate to your final destination at no extra charge. This is the perfect opportunity for those of you who did not want to pay for a second bag, didn't want to have to go to the baggage claim carrousel, or who just do not want to deal with the overhead bin space inside the airplane. It's so much better flying with no bags to carry, especially to those airports I mentioned before with fly stairs.

Once your group or number has been called, you are ready to board your flight. Aren't you excited? All you need is your boarding pass, unless you are flying internationally, and then a passport with your photo ready is required to board. See? It was easy.

As you make your way to the airplane and wait to get in, look at your boarding pass one more time and locate your seat number. Be ready. Take this opportunity to remove anything from your bag that you may need immediately; a book, your travel blankets, etc. Do not wait to be in the middle of the aisle to find your seat number or to retrieve a magazine from inside your bag. Remember that there are others behind you waiting as well. Be polite.

CHAPTER 6

INSIDE THE METAL TUBE

There are so many stories about how people act inside an airplane that this guide is not enough. While I will try to tell you how we should act inside this metal tube and show you the different examples of airplane etiquette we should all follow, I will tell you stories that you may not believe are true. Unless you work in this industry or actually witness any these situations, your jaw will drop often frequently throughout the whole chapter. Just watch for flies.

Now that the hard part is behind you and you are safely on board, one of your main concerns is going to be comfort. Let's imagine you've finally found your seat, and it is a window seat in the middle of the cabin. Depending on the airline, you may or may not have plenty of space for your sexy legs.

Remember when I said dress comfortably? Also dress appropriately for your flight. I know you may be going to the Caribbean, but if I can see your boobs almost completely or your shorts are so short we can almost see your private parts, please don't demand we turn down the air conditioning because you alone are cold. If you think the temperature is too cold or too hot you can always ask a crew member to change the temperature or even to ask others next to you if is really cold or hot. Maybe you are just having a private summer. Who knows? Ask nicely, however. If you ask rudely to change the temperature, guess what the flight attendant is going to do? Exactly; absolutely nothing.

Now, let's talk about going to the restrooms as soon as you come aboard. You waited all this time outside in the terminal. You had plenty of time to use the much bigger and more comfortable bathroom outside, but no; you waited to use the tiny and not so clean restroom inside. If you came running like a cheetah from your connecting flight, then I forgive you. Those tiny restrooms inside the aircraft are not the cleanest you will find, especially between flights. Have you ever seen how they are cleaned? The cleaning crews come and do a good but very quick job of sanitizing the bathrooms inside an airplane. Sometimes you can still smell the pee from other customers from weeks ago. Try to avoid these restrooms as much as possible, unless you have no choice on a long flight. I can only imagine my dear ladies trying to use an airplane bathroom and trying not to touch anything at the same time. Gross.

Always say hello to the flight attendant up front, especially when we are saying hello to you. It is rude to ignore us as we welcome you aboard. I try to say hi to everyone if I am not busy. It is very hard to miss a six-foot-tall flight attendant who is looking at you and talking to you. Still, some people totally ignore me as I welcome them into my office. I remember a flight from Boston to Los Angeles many years ago. A young lady, probably still in her teens, wearing a short dress, big, dark sunglasses, and a leopard hat came on board with what was clearly a fake name brand purse with the fake rollaboard to match. I welcomed her on board as I do everyone. She not only ignored me, but she also dropped her big rollaboard at my feet, turned her face and went to her seat back in economy. I remember the guy seated in row one asking,

"Did she really do that?"

"Yes, she did". I responded.

I immediately stopped boarding. After I got her attention, I asked her what she wanted me to do with her bag. Pointing with her finger she said,

"That, here."

At that point the conversation was over. I took her bag and put it outside to be gate checked.

There many rules and regulations dictated by the FAA in the US or in any other country, depending on your airline. Some are stricter than others. Unfortunately, we all have to follow those rules to have a safe and pleasant flight. Now, some flight attendants take those rules and regulations more seriously than others. I truly believe that the way you say things may get you a better outcome, and a smile may get you even better results. Remember, we deal with hundreds of different people every day we fly. Some are nice, and some are not so nice. As a passenger, one of the reasons I do not like to sit in front of a bulkhead is because I have to put everything up. Not even my backpack can stay. This is just for take-off and landing, but it is very annoying to me and, I am sure, to many of you, as well. As a traveler, I understand your frustration, but as a flight attendant I have to follow those rules and explain to customers that they must keep their rows clear of bags or any personal belongings. Most people understand and are ok with it. Usually, people who fly often know this, while those who aren't frequent flyers don't. I often have to repeat myself several times before I almost have to grab the bags myself. Of course, what usually follows is a look so nasty I can almost feel the daggers in my back.

For the rest of the cabin, all bags have to be completely under the seat in front of you. This is the way it is in almost all the world's airlines, and it's an easy rule to follow. We not only mention this in our safety demonstration, but we say it again while we go through the cabin. You wouldn't believe how many times I have to tell someone to push their bag completely under the seat. We do not want to tell you any more than you want to hear us saying it, but there are reasons why we all have to comply with this. Not only is it a federal regulation, but it is also for our own safety. What if the aircraft were on fire; an airplane made of metal and plastic and full of fuel. It's certainly happened before. Now imagine what can happen and how fast. Every second counts during an emergency evacuation. If there is a bag obstructing you and the passenger sitting next to you, it can prevent you from exiting the burning aircraft on time. Now do you see why we have this rule?

The seatbelt rule is one of those rules that you may think everyone follows, for obvious reasons, but they don't. But just like in your car when you travel, seatbelts need to be on, both for your safety and the safety of that poor person you are going to hit with one of your body parts. All customers have to be seated with their seatbelts fastened before we can even push back from the gate, at least in the US. The cabin has to be "secured' before we can tell the Captain we are ready for departure.

Some people hate to be told anything, especially by someone they do not know. Maybe you are the CEO of a huge company on Wall Street or you just do not like people telling you what to do. Then don't wait for me to pass by you and tell you several times to put your seatbelts on. Be an adult.

During turbulence it is very important that everybody, including the crew, stay in their seats and wait. I truly believe it is a psychological thing that as soon as the seatbelt light goes on, ten people want to go to the bathroom. Seriously? The captain just told us all to stay seated. He also happens to have very high-tech radar in front of him, so he knows what's coming. If you see the flight attendants taking their seats during turbulence, that is a good indication you should be doing the same thing. It means the shit is going to get ugly soon.

During one trip to Boston we were actually very close to landing and I was in the back of the cabin. The captain called us to tell us to sit down because there was bad weather right in front of us, and then he was going to inform the passengers. I got my galley ready; I put everything away, took my seat, and put on my seatbelt as soon as I could. I heard the captain telling everyone on the P.A. system to stay seated with their seatbelts on because bad weather was ahead of us. He told all flight attendants to remain seated as well. What would you do if you heard that? You would stay in your seat, wouldn't you? I think this lady, who was probably in her mid-sixties, must have heard the complete opposite. As the airplane started to shake, sometimes very strongly, she decided to stand up to go to the bathroom. As she approached me in my seat I told her to stay seated because it was not safe to be walking around the cabin. The turbulence got really bad. We had a couple of drops and people were screaming in unison, like they do on a rollercoaster at an amusement park. It was bad. Still, she completely ignored me and decided to keep walking back. As she got closer to the one of the restrooms, a really bad drop happened, and I could see her whole body lift off the floor for a couple of seconds and then drop like a sack of potatoes on the floor. She definitely got hurt, I thought. She was screaming, "Help!" while people seated around her were trying to hold her hands. There was nothing I could do other than to stay seated as well. My safety was as important as the rest of the passengers' safety, and I was not going to take a risk because some lady ignored orders and decided to do whatever she wanted. As soon as everything was calm I asked her if she was fine. The first thing that came out of her mouth was, "I am going to sue this company, the whole crew and you for not helping me". At that point there was nothing I could say. She was mad, but she had it coming. She got up, went to the restroom, and then returned to her seat. I could not wait for all the paperwork that she was going to make me do now. I figured she wasn't kidding, and I had to protect myself. I never heard anything more about that incident, however.

Now, it is true that sometimes the pilots may forget to turn the seatbelt sign off but asking a crew if it's ok to unbuckle is not going to cost you anything. The flight attendant may or may not call the captain to check; maybe he just forgot.

Often during a flight, passengers will ask me if they can get up, either to use the facilities or just to look for something in their bags. Let me explain something; I will make it as easy to understand as possible. When the seatbelt sign is on and you ask a flight attendant if you can get up, they will never say YES. Their response will be,

"I just need to remind you that the seatbelt sign is on."

If you paid very close attention to the response, you will notice that at no time did they say NO. The flight attendant is just doing their job according to FAA regulations. If you decide to get up, we won't fight you or have you arrested. We did our job. We have to remind all passenger about their seatbelts when the sign is on, at all times. Do not take it personally.

Sometimes there are little "friends" who decide to smuggle themselves inside the cabin without any permission from us. This can happen because many destinations are not as clean as they could be. You should see the way some of the terminals look! Often it is very hot and humid, which is the perfect condition for some of those friends looking for refuge inside the aircraft. We were almost done boarding from one of our beloved Caribbean cities once, and we were almost ready to close the doors, when suddenly a loud scream got everyone's attention:

"A COCKROACH!"

It was almost like that scene from the movie Airplane, when the flight attendant announced that there was no more coffee. After the initial scream, there was total silence for a few seconds, and then others started to scream as well. It was total chaos. I'm a pretty tough guy, but I'm not a fan of any bugs, especially roaches. The captain came to the back as soon as he heard the noise. Suddenly, the big flying insect landed very close to the first row, right between the handle and the space we use to hold on to when walking around the cabin. The captain jumped backwards, and I swear I heard a little squeaking noise coming out of him. Nobody, not even the captain, wanted to be close to the insect. There was calm for about 30 seconds, then the flying roach took off heading toward the middle of the cabin. I saw big men scream like little girls and try to flee from the horrible creature. We had to get out; there was no other way. It was like a funny scene from a horror movie, with people screaming and running for their lives, just because of a roach. Everybody had to go inside the terminal and the flight was delayed. I have no idea if they actually fumigated the cabin or took the roach out, but we were back inside and ready to go home two hours later.

CHAPTER 7

AIR MARSHALS

After the tragic incident on 9-11, security at airports and on airplanes got tighter. I started to see more air marshals on airplanes, especially on some routes. When I tell you that you will have no clue who they are, trust me; you won't. They can be a man or a woman, someone older or younger, or even that sexy lady you have been trying to hook up with for the past hour. They are completely incognito, but they are armed. I used to see them coming to the airplane first, making it really obvious who they were. Sometimes other passengers would ask me why they were boarding first. I used to tell them they were airline employees. That started to change, however, and now they board with the rest of the passengers. The crew knows who they are, though, including the pilots and all flight attendants. All armed individuals inside the airplane have to know where each other is seated. This includes not only air marshals, but also secret service and FBI agents and members of any other federal agency. Police officers cannot board an airplane armed, but they are of great help in some situations.

Air marshals will have specific seats assigned by their office; they can't just take any seats they want. If you ask someone to change seats and that person says no, do not assume he or she is an asshole. They may be an air marshal. Of course, it could be that he or she really is just an asshole…

In any case, DO NOT EVER ask someone if there are air marshals on the airplane. Just don't do it. They are there for a reason; to protect us all.

CHAPTER 8

INTERNATIONAL FLYING

I do a lot of international flying for work and just to have fun and learn about the world. It is a big world and airplanes can help you get there faster.

A very important document we all need when we travel internationally is a passport. You will need one of those to travel the world. I can remember when I could travel to Canada and Mexico with only my driver's license. Not anymore.

Make sure your passport is up to date. One of the common mistakes travelers make when going on international trips is not signing their passport. Did you know that until you sign your passport, it is actually not valid? Do not forget; forgetting to sign your passport can get you in trouble, especially if your customs officer is in a really bad mood. Also, make sure you have the right visa for the country you are visiting, if you need one. Many places have restrictions depending on where you are coming from or where your passport is from. Countries like Costa Rica or Colombia will ask if you have a return ticket or an exit way out of the country. This is also for US citizens and European citizens. For example, if you are traveling to Colombia and then continuing to Machu Pichu in Peru, before you enter the airplane in the US they will ask for your ticket from Colombia to Peru. If you are just taking a bus, then you have to show them proof of that. It is always a good idea to check the website of the embassy in the country you are visiting or just ask on social media for more information.

If you are a permanent resident of the US, but you have a passport from another country, you still may need a visa to visit your vacation spot. If you are flying to Europe or through Europe, make sure you are familiar with all requirements of the Schengen Agreement, which was created on June 14th, 1985 near the town of Schengen, Luxembourg. The first countries on the list were France, Germany, Belgium, Luxembourg, and Netherlands. In later years more countries were added to the list. Basically, the Agreement abolished passports and other border controls at their mutual border nations. With a US passport you won't need a visa to travel between these countries if you are staying for less than ninety days. If you have another country's passport you may check to see if you need a visa. All this may change periodically.

It is very important when you are traveling internationally to get to the airport on time. Airlines usually close international flights earlier than regular flights. They have to be checked by Customs of that country as well, and the list of all passengers on board must be checked, too.

Now that you are on the airplane, get ready for arrival at your international destination. Even if you have an US or European passport, you may have to fill out the immigration and customs forms for the country you are visiting. When I am on a flight to Mexico City and I'm about to give people their form, you have no idea how many people say,

"No, I'm American."

My response is always the same, said with a smile:

"Exactly, take one."

We Americans are not exempt from filling out customs and immigration forms when we travel. We are not that special.

Here is a lesson from International Travel 101: BRING YOUR OWN PEN. Airlines will not provide you with a pen to fill out your forms. You have to bring your own or ask your neighbor to borrow one. Don't forget; it has to be blue or black ink.

Immigration forms are self-explanatory. Read the damned form before you start writing whatever it is you feel like writing! I often have a little fun by answering passengers with a little sarcasm and getting away with it. For example, people will often ask me,

"What passport number do I put here?"

I will respond:

"6452376..." and keep creating some passport number until they figure out how foolish that question was. If they ask me what name to write, I will start spelling my own name.

It is also very interesting to see how some destinations are more "high maintenance" than others. In some cities I will pass out the forms right away. A few people may ask for another form because they made mistakes; no big deal - we are all human. In other cities, like Bogota, Colombia, you have to wait until almost landing to give them the forms. First of all, I love Colombia; I used to live in Bogota for a couple of years and I am married to a Colombian. I am still trying to figure out why every time I work a Bogota flight, the flight attendant call button will ding over and over because almost everyone has made a mistake on the form. It is almost out of control - every flight, every time. After the fourth time I give you a form, something must be wrong with you. READ BEFORE YOU WRITE.

If you can't find a pen to fill out your form, don't worry. There will be pens and fresh forms available to you before you enter the country you are visiting. Usually there will be tables set up with all the forms and pens you need. How difficult it is to bring a pen? Just make your life easier.

If you are coming to the US from some beautiful island in the Caribbean or visiting from Europe, and you are connecting on another flight right afterwards to another city or country, know that ALL FLIGHTS arriving to the US on ANY carrier will have to do

Immigration and Customs at the first city port of arrival. That means you have to pass Immigration, pick up all your luggage, and go through Customs before giving your bags to an airline representative, who is usually waiting for you as soon as you exit Customs. On almost all flights that I work coming to the US, someone always tries to argue with me about this same thing. "They sent my bags to the final destination before," they will say.

Now, perhaps when leaving the US Continent your airline and country of connection may have different rules and regulations. For example, on a vacation to Thailand, which is one of my favorite places in the world, not only for its beauty but also for its people and culinary experience, I had to make a stop for several hours in Dubai. Not only I did not have to go through Customs in Dubai, they also sent my luggage all the way to Thailand.

Rules also apply to those four bottles of rum you were drinking the whole week during your recent Jamaican beach vacation. You liked it so much you wanted to share it with your friends and family at home. You carried the box with the bottles inside all the way from Jamaica and now you have landed in the US with plenty of time before your next connecting flight home on the same airline. After you pass Customs and you are almost free to go, you have to give all your bags, already tagged, to your airline representative to be sent to your final destination. Guess what? You may have to go to the checkpoint again and pass TSA before heading to your gate. You carried your four bottles of rum all the way from Jamaica only for them to be taken by a lovely TSA agent because there are more than 3.4 ounces and the duty-free box is not a "sealed approved" bag or container. Usually those bags are plastic and sealed with a green happy face up front. Your rum is now an amazing gift to the Unites States Government; I'm sure they will appreciate it. There is a solution for this, however. Before you give your bags again to the airline rep after you exit Customs, you should put your bottles inside your checked bag. This is the time to put inside your bags any items that you may think will not pass the checkpoint. Now you may enjoy another glass of rum when you get home that night.

People get fined all the time because of crap they bring or try to bring through Customs. If you know you can't bring a banana, don't bring the banana. It's still a fruit and fruit is not allowed.

Coming back to the US can also be a pain, especially at some airports. One of my favorite tools is Global Entry. I always say that it was the best $100 I ever spent. There are assigned kiosks and Customs lines for Global Entry holders. I can't tell you how many times I have seen long Immigration and Customs lines after a long flight. You can avoid those lines with Global Entry. If you are a US Citizen or a lawful resident of the US, you are eligible for Global Entry, and Canadians may take advantage of Global entry benefits through membership in the NEXUS program. Surprisingly, citizens of other countries may take advantage of the Global Entry program as well, but with a few additional requirements. This may change, but you can check their website for updated information about this program at CBP.GOV. Don't want to spend that money or don't travel that much? There is also a free government app you can download to your phone called Mobile Passport, which is absolutely free of charge.

The use of cellphones and cameras is prohibited in almost all airports I have visited, including in the United States when you are going through Customs and Immigration. Just don't do it. Depending on what country and airport you are arriving at, it may be the last time you see your cellphone. They will either take it from you or give you a fine, so just don't do it. If you really have to send a text, be smart. Look around before they come and embarrass you in front of everyone.

CHAPTER 9

CABIN ETIQUETTE

Cabin etiquette is something we should all know about when we fly. There are no rules and no bible we must follow for behaving or interacting with others inside an airplane, but our common sense should kick in and everything should be fine…or so we think.

Good fliers are almost ready; they know what they are doing. They get their drinks when we are passing out drinks or a meal when it is time for meal service. Others are totally clueless, however. Here are some of the biggest trouble areas when it comes to a lack of etiquette:

ARM RESTS:

Sitting in the middle seat is a bad enough experience, especially if the person next to you is a bit large. When you are sitting in the middle seat, you get to have both arm rests. They are all yours.

LARGE PASSENGERS:

This is something that we have to be careful about to make sure we don't hurt anybody's feelings. If you are heavy enough to occupy two seats, please buy two seats. You and I know how big you are. I am very sorry for whatever the reason is for you being this large but making another person's trip miserable is an asshole move. Always ask the agents outside or one of the flight attendants whether you can get a better seat for you or the person you are completely crushing.

RECLINING SEATS:

This is a subject that many people have gotten completely wrong. There are some airlines whose seats do not recline; if you are flying on one of those airlines, you don't have to worry about any of this drama. Usually, if you are seated in front of one of the emergency exit doors, there is a possibility that your seat won't recline. Pushing and pushing your seat back won't fix anything. Don't get angry, at least not with the crew. Remember how I told you that being nice would get you far? You can always ask a flight attendant for a better seat. If the flight is not full they may give it to you. On almost all airlines, the seats in front of the exit rows do not recline. Many airlines may tell you this when you purchase your ticket, either on the phone or on their website.

If you are seated in a reclining seat, you should only put the seat back after the drink and meal service has ended, if offered. Think about it, and don't do anything you don't want people to do to you. After the service is done, recline slowly. Look back first and be careful. Be gentle; someone's laptop could be right behind you, or even a hot drink.

BAG PLACEMENT:

Always try to put your bag close to your seat when possible. If you are someone who waits until the end and decides to come in with two bags, you may not get that space you were hoping for. It is always ok to move other passengers' bags aside to accommodate yours, but never move another person's bag to another bin in order to put your rollaboard in it. If you can't find space, ask a flight attendant for help. Also, put your own bag up. You brought it all the way from home, so *you* put it up. Suddenly you can't carry your own bag? I'm sure they can check it for you to your final destination. When placing a bag under the seat in front of you, make sure it fits. Do not block the other person and do not hog the overhead bin. It is not a private flight on which you are the only passenger. Place only one bag on top and the smallest bag under your seat. If you can put your bag with the wheels or handles facing the aisle, do so. That may save some space for others. Remember, this is shared space.

On a flight from South Florida to San Francisco one time, an elderly couple was seated in the second row. They were traveling very light and the gentleman put a very small package and a fedora hat in the overhead bin, and nothing more. Then he closed it, even though the bin was totally empty. Around mid-boarding the gentleman seated in row one came on board and, as federal regulations stated, all bags have to go up if you are seated in front of the bulkhead. He knew this, but there was no more space up front, as this was a very full flight. He only had a large sport bag pack. I remembered the space next to the hat belonging to the couple right behind him. As I opened the bin to place the bag, the gentleman in row two decided to tell me very aggressively to not touch his stuff. I was as surprised as everyone else around us witnessing this little discussion. I told him I needed the space and I was very careful of his hat. He got up very abruptly, almost pushing me out of the way, closed the bin and told me that was his bin, his space. I didn't know whether to start laughing or call security. They could have been my grandparents, and I know how some grandparents are. I told him not to touch me again and explained that the bin was for everyone to share. I also told him he could lease a private jet with the promise that nobody would bother him or put anything next to their belongings. At that point he had two choices; to stay in his seat and be respectful of the crew or take the next flight to San Francisco. He was furious and asked for my name. I showed him my name tag and spelled it out for him, B O R I S, with a great smile of course. After many tries to get me to give him my full name and employee number, and after threatening to call the company, he decided to stay seated and watch his tv monitor for the rest of the flight until his wife paid me a visit later to apologize for him.

GETTING UP:

If you are seated in the window seat and you need to use the restroom, it is totally ok to do so. Just very gently tap the other person's shoulder and say,

"Excuse me".

That's all you need to do. Try to stand as seldom as possible, unless you are in the aisle seat. Have you seen those people that are constantly getting up to get something from the overhead bin? That's very annoying; especially if you leave it open every time.

WINDOW SHADES:

If you decide to purchase a window seat, you have total control over the window shade. Unfortunately, many airplanes flying around still do not have the technology others have to control the windows from the front. If you are not sure, you can always ask your seat mates if they prefer the windows closed or open. They probably won't care anyway. You can offer to switch seats if they do. When the cabin is dark and everyone is still sleeping because it was the first flight in the morning, don't be that person who has the only open window on the cabin; especially if the sun is coming through full blast. It's very annoying to be on an airplane when everyone is trying to sleep, and the cabin is dark, when suddenly some asshole opens his window and a full ray of light comes in, illuminating the whole cabin that just a moment ago was very comfy and dark. What are you trying to do, look for rainbows at 3700 feet? Do you think that a flying unicorn may pass by? Close the window shade and let the other passengers relax.

ARGUING WITH THE CREW:

As you can see, there are so many rules you need to follow when you travel by air. Your flight attendants did not create those rules, but it is their job to make sure we all follow them. Arguing with a cabin crew member will get you kicked off the flight so fast you will never see it coming. If you know you have to put your tray table up for take-off and landing, just do it. It is very annoying when we have to tell you several times; in the end you have to do it anyway. The same goes for electronics. Flights often take off late because of an unruly passenger acting like a two-year-old child. You may encounter Lovely Betsy, who has been a flight attendant since 1955 but left her good work manners with her personality back in the 1980s. Trust me; they are out there, so do not argue. Just take their name and contact the airline. Telling you seven times to turn your laptop off is not rude.

ODORS:

This is another very delicate subject, but unfortunately it is part of our travel etiquette when we fly. Many cultures around the world may have a peculiar smell or traditional odor. It may be wonderful to your partner or family members, who are probably used to your odor, but it's not wonderful for the general public when you travel. You know you stink; others have probably told you before. Try to take a shower before you head to the airport and use deodorant. It's as simple as that. I understand that you are going backpacking around the world and you may not have showers in the middle of the Amazon, but I am very sure you have time to take a shower. It's just very aggravating for people around you, stuck inside a metal tube with recycled air, to smell your four months of jungle travels. I had a couple of European guys on one of my flights, who were both seated in the middle seat in the back of the cabin. You could tell they had not had a shower or bath for at least three weeks. I could smell them from the front of the cabin. One of the ladies next to them came to me and asked me very gently if there was another seat for her. I knew exactly why. She was so nice and didn't want to be rude about it. Fortunately, I had empty seats in the front and I gave her an upgrade. It was not fair for her to smell that for the whole flight. The same goes for perfumes and colognes. If you just bought that cologne on sale at some store for $3, it may be awesome for you, but not for the rest of the world. Do not bathe in cheap cologne before your flight. I have seen passengers taken off of flights because of their odor. Oh yeah; I almost forgot. Please keep your socks on!

LAVATORY:

I get shivers just thinking about this. Let's face it; lavatories on airplanes are disgusting. Airlines need to keep the lavatory as clean as possible before every flight, so be respectful. Try to keep it as clean as you can for the next person. It is not your personal bathroom, and others are probably waiting to use it as well. Lavatories are unisex, for both males and females. Do not spend more than 20 minutes in the lavatory.

You should also know that joining the Mile-High Club is prohibited. Airplane bathrooms are small, so I give you an A for creativity. If you want to have sex inside a lavatory on an airplane, you'd better take a good shower as soon as you get to your hotel or home. Lavatories are full of germs. It is not only inappropriate to do this, but it's also very yucky.

EXERCISE / YOGA:

This is not the right time to practice any of the new yoga poses you just learned from your yogi best friend, or to practice the new exercise routines your trainer told you to do this week. Mind other people's spaces, including your crew's. Nobody needs to see the little hole you have on your yoga pants right between your two butt cheeks. Jumping in the middle of the aisle is not only annoying, it's also dangerous, especially to the people sitting around you. Cabin galleys are the flight attendants' work space. It's also the only space they have away from passengers. Sometimes, depending on the type of aircraft, it's the only place to have a meal. They don't need to have your ass right on top of their food. Use your common sense. Would you like me to go to your cubicle and start exercising or doing yoga while you are working? Feel free to walk around the cabin and stretch your legs in the aisle, just be careful with passengers around you.

KIDS KICKING YOUR SEAT:

This is another subject that causes many very ugly arguments while flying. If a kid is kicking the back of your seat, be patient. First give the parents the international "that is annoying" look. Just look back and smile; they may take the hint. If nothing happens, very politely ask the parent if they could stop their kid from doing that. A smile can be very helpful in these cases. If nothing is done, ask a flight attendant for help, very nicely. Even if the kid is a pain in the ass, parents don't like others to scold their kids. This may cause a very ugly situation for everyone involved.

CONVERSATIONS:

You'd be very surprised by what people talk about with others on airplanes. It is absolutely ok to talk to the person next to you, but if you see that person ready to go to sleep or opening a laptop to do some work, they probably won't like to hear about how your ex just slept with your best friend or to see pictures of Candy, your pet iguana. You may be going on vacation with your girlfriends to Cancun and you are already in a party mood. Very nice, but not everyone around you is traveling for the same reason. Not everyone around you needs to know about the last time you had your period, or that you had sex with your mother's pool boy. It is rude. Keep it to yourself. This also applies to gentlemen, as well. Enjoy your Bloody Mary but keep your stories to yourself and to your friend next to you. Turn down the volume. If people are already giving you the look, respect them. If I can hear you from the front galley, you are probably being too loud. This goes for those trying to talk on the phone, too. Keep it to yourself. Many airlines now have Wi-Fi, and you may be able to use phone applications like WhatsApp. Text all you want but using them to make phone calls is another story. This is one of the gray areas in the FAA regulations as it is a very new technology. Many airlines may prohibit you from making voice calls while flying. Respect that.

ALCOHOL:

This is the number one reason people get kicked off of flights and it's also caused many unplanned landings around the world. According to the Civil Aviation Authority (CAA) in the UK, the low air pressure associated with flying effectively thins the blood and theoretically strengthens the effect of alcohol. Some doctors say it is hypoxia that makes you feel more drunk, caused by the amount of oxygen getting into your blood because of the cabin altitude and pressure. Whatever the reason is, some people just get crazy when they drink on airplanes. Drink in moderation, especially if you know drinking makes you dance or be mean to others.

SIGNS:

Respect the signs. If the seatbelt sign is on is for a reason, respect that. It is not only for your safety, but for the safety of those around you.

CALL BUTTON:

Flight attendants have to serve many other passengers on that same flight. Do not press that button just because you are finished and want your trash to be taken away. Just wait. They will pass through the cabin collecting all trash at once after they are done with service. Think about everything you need before you call the flight attendants for something. They are not your personal servants. If you need a soda with ice and another snack, ask for it at the same time. Don't wait for the flight attendant to bring you the soda and then ask for the snack. They are probably busy. Always be careful when handling the trash – and don't drop it on your neighbor.

CHAPTER 10

KIDS ON THE FLIGHT

I usually love kids. Their cuteness can make anybody's heart melt, especially when they are babies, and the majority of kids on flights behave pretty reasonably. Hey, they are children. With some kids, however, I just want to open the window and throw them out. No, just kidding.

When you are traveling with your kids always remember one thing; they are completely yours. You are the one who decided to start a family. You love your kids, and so do I, but they are yours. You are as responsible for your kids on the airplane as you are at home. Some parents truly believe that at the moment they enter the aircraft, their responsibilities stop. I hate to have to break it to them, but they are wrong. This is a transportation company, not a babysitting service.

The first thing you should do at home is pack all food, diapers, and everything else you may need for your baby. Do not expect your airline or the airport to get any of that for you.

Not long ago, during one of my regular flights, I heard the call button, so I went to see what the passenger needed. It was a mother with an infant. I had helped her at the beginning of the flight to get an extra seat for her and the baby, so they could be more comfortable. Before we proceed with the story, I want to make sure all parents out there are clear about sitting with infants. If your child is under two years old, they can sit on your lap completely free of charge. Kids over two years old need to have their own seat and to stay seated with their seatbelts for takeoff and landing. If you are traveling with a car seat and you did not purchase a seat, then you may pick the car seat up when you get to your final destination. Sometimes, when the flights are not full, the ground crew or the inflight crew will try to accommodate you, so you can travel a little more comfortably with your baby. If the flight is full there is nothing we can do. I can't tell you how many times parents try to get into fights with crew members because there is someone sitting next to them or they found out there is an extra seat and the car seat has already gone to the belly of the plane. If the crew can find an extra seat for you and your child, be thankful. Anyway, when I got to their seat, the mother asked me if I had baby formula, to which I immediately responded NO. The woman had very light skin - almost pink, with very beautiful, long red hair almost covering the tv of the passenger behind her. The baby was probably around six or seven months old. The mother turned red; so red that I became worried and asked her if she was ok. She went ballistic and started accusing the airline and me of horrible customer service and demanding to know how in hell I did not have baby formula for her infant. I apologized to her and told her again that airlines, especially in the US, usually did not offer baby food, especially not baby formula. Now she had the attention of everyone around her. She was very loud. You could see others taking their headsets off, so they could witness the spectacle.

"What am I supposed to give her?" she said. "She is hungry, and I have to feed her. This totally f***** up" she repeated again and again.

I tried to calm her down, even sitting on the seat next to her so nobody else could hear me. She was crying and sobbing like a little girl whose daddy just told her she had to do her homework. Others around her were trying to calm her as well. I offered some apple juice and whatever we had on the airplane. I actually felt bad for her, but there was nothing I could do. She did not prepare for her and her baby to travel accordingly. Thank God we only had a couple of minutes left on the flight.

It is so important to make sure you are ready when you travel with kids. But also remember that there will be others around you. One of the most annoying things, not only to me, but for other passengers, is when parents decide that it is an extremely good idea to bring toys that make noise. I even had a kid with a small piano once. Flying next to a couple of kids playing their marimba or their very loud video games is absolutely irritating. Bringing video games or tablets for them to play with is absolutely a very smart idea, but you also should bring very good headsets. There are many types of very cool headsets for small kids. Trying to get them to use them before the flights is also a good plan. If you child is completely into their video games, tv show or whatever it is keeping them entertained, LEAVE THEM ALONE. If they are hungry they will tell you. Sometimes I really don't know who the kid is by the way some parents behave. Sometimes the kids are complete angels and the parents are the ones who are loud and obnoxious.

Kids also react differently to weather related movements of the plane. Some may get a little sick, while others don't. If it is a short flight, do not give them more food they can't handle. If they wouldn't eat something at home, don't give it to them on the airplane. Just because the sodas are free, it is not a good idea to give four cans in less than 15 minutes to your child, accompanied by three bags of pretzels and five chocolate chip cookies. Guess where all that is going to end up while you are landing, with the help of pressure changes and airplane movement due to some clouds? Exactly!

Keep your kids as quiet as possible and keep them entertained. If your technique at home is to ignore them while they are throwing a tantrum, this is not a good time to do the same. You cannot just let them do whatever they want.

I once had a couple with an infant who were extremely messy, to say the least. At the end of the flight their aisle looked like several bags of food had exploded everywhere. There was trash and even a dirty diaper on the seat. As they were leaving they could tell we were surprised by all the mess they had created in just couple of hours. My colleague and I were really upset, as this would delay the return flight until the ground crew could thoroughly clean up that mess. The father turned to my fellow crew member and told her,

"Sorry, it was the baby."

I didn't know what to say. In any case, it was probably better for me to just stay quiet as I probably would have said something I would regret. My dear colleague had other plans, however. She almost immediately told them with a very firm voice:

"Who is the adult here?" She asked. "This is just disgusting," she continued, as she went to the back galley to vent even more.

They did not say anything or even try to pick up some of the garbage on the floor and all over the seats. We did make them take the dirty diaper.

I often see parents and sometimes single parents traveling with kids and many bags. I understand that with the price of checking bags these days you want to save some money and bring everything you own on board. Put everything you need for your child, especially infants, in a single bag. You should check the rest of your big bags at the ticket counter or even at the gate. Take advantage of the free bag check the majority of airlines offer at the gate. Even if they don't offer, always ask the agent or the flight attendant when you come in; there is a very high possibility they will try to help you. This way you can pay more attention to your kids and it eases the stress on you. It is your decision to do this, however. Do not expect others to help you when you don't want to help yourself. When you travel with kids you should take all the help that is offered to you, especially with heavy luggage. Imagine getting to your destination and not having to deal with carrying bags and being free to simply take care of your kids. It is totally worth it.

While on a flight you may encounter passengers who, for some reason, have very little patience with younger customers. They see a kid and it's like they saw Jason from Friday the 13th. It does not matter if the kids are good or bad; they just won't sit near them. When this happens, it can be very embarrassing for the parents. Some of these people will suddenly demand free upgrades and better seats on the plane as if they were allergic to children. In these cases, I try my best to give the person another seat or to upgrade the parents, instead. They wouldn't want to sit next to such a horrible person anyway. I'm not a fan of kids when I am on vacation and I am simply looking for peace and tranquility, but to express your feelings about kids in that manner, especially in front of their parents, is not very polite. If you can't fly when kids are around, and you honestly can't stand crying or the sound of children playing, you are going to have problems. Try to avoid flying during the holidays, during the summer flying, or flying to family destinations. As a matter of fact, do what I told the customer from San Francisco; get a private jet. An elderly lady threw a tantrum on one of my flights because of the number of kids on the flight. She would not shut up about it the whole flight to Orlando, Florida; home of Mickey Mouse.

The diaper situation is another big problem. Parents need to make sure they handle this issue at the right place and time. Obviously, you may have to change that full and smelly diaper at some point, especially on a long flight, but there is a place you can do it without causing any problems: the lavatory. Almost all airplane lavatories today are equipped with changing tables – there is at least one on every flight, and they are there for a reason. We all know you love your cute baby and you are probably used to all of the smells that come out of him or her, but the people around you may find it repulsive when you decide to change the baby on a tray table or on the seat next to you. Really? You want to use the tray tables to change a diaper? The same place where people put their drinks and food? That's extremely unsanitary. Think about it for a second and then remember what I said. It is your baby, and he or she is adorable, but that baby is still only yours, and not everyone else's.

Unaccompanied minors are one of my favorite type of customers. They are so cute, flying by themselves to see their divorced mom or dad or even their grandparents for summer vacation. These little ones (and sometime even the ones who are not so little) have to pay an extra fee to have the entire crew function as a babysitter. I have to say that the majority of minors traveling alone are very well-behaved and follow the rules at all times. Sometimes you may have a pair of twins on a red eye flight from California jumping and screaming for five hours in the middle of the night, not only making all of the people around them hate children for that time period but making every single member of the crew want to cry intensively.

Personally, I would not send my seven-year-old daughter by herself on a flight to see her other side of the family, but that is just me. I don't know what type of weirdo may wind up sitting next to her.

Flight attendants and other airline employees who have contact with a minor traveling alone take very good care of them. I usually try to sit them together if there are more than one traveling. I will also try my best to seat them next to an empty seat or in a row by themselves. I treat them as though they were my kids.

If you are sending your little ones off by themselves on a flight, especially to international destinations, get them ready. Give them a small bag in which they can keep all of their entertainment, such as video games, books, coloring books and headsets (remember we spoke about those earlier?). Don't send them off with any toys that make noise.

Make sure you talk to your child about their behavior on the plane, using whatever tricks you may have, and tell them to pay very close attention to the flight attendants and to do what they are told to do on the flight. We are totally responsible for your kids while they are flying, and we want them to have a comfortable and safe flight. Traveling with your kids can be stressful, but it can also be easy. You are the parent; you are the adult. Do not rely on others to teach your kids how to behave. That is your job. Pay attention to them, but do not overreact and, most importantly, leave them alone if they are quiet and enjoying the moment.

CHAPTER 11

PETS AND MORE PETS.

This is another very sensitive subject. It is also the reason for countless delays. These days, everyone wants to travel with their pets.

Airlines have different rules regarding pet policies, depending on the company, flag and destination. Regulations regarding pets change almost too frequently and there are so many that it would be impossible to list them all here. Always plan ahead. Call your airline and ask them about their rules regarding pets, including service and emotional support animals.

A regular pet is an animal you decided to adopt or purchase for you or your family to enjoy. They do not have any other job than to love you and to be there when you come home. Even though you love really Lulu the Pomeranian, since she is a regular pet, you will have to pay a fee to travel with her in the cabin and sometimes, depending on the airline, in the cargo hold.

A service animal is trained to do a job or to perform a task for people with disabilities, according to the Americans with Disabilities Act, or ADA. Service animals are trained to help the blind and people with limited mobility, or even as a medical alert.

The most common service animals you will see on an airplane are dogs. A long time ago I had a very small monkey on a flight that was traveling with a very young girl and her family. I was shocked by the idea of a monkey on board an airplane. I remember the mother telling me that even though the monkey was for home activities only, this was a relocation for them, so they had no choice. As it was a service animal, she could bring the monkey with her as permitted by my airline back then.

At my airline we only accept dogs and cats as service or emotional support animals. You will not be allowed to bring your emotional support goldfish or donkey on board my airline or any other. This is why it is so important to check with the airline first and determine the required documentation you may need to bring with you when you get to the airport with Cleo, your emotional support snake.

To have a legal emotional support animal (EAS), you have to be considered emotionally "disabled" by a licensed mental health professional, like a psychiatrist, therapist, etc. as evidenced by a proper prescription letter. Even if you can bring more than one EAS animal on board, there are many restrictions regarding this. Your animal can't be a threat to other animals, passengers or crew. If Lulu decides to bark extremely loudly and growl at other pets and people, she may have to stay with you until she calms down and you may miss your flight. Pets that are violent or physically distressed may not be able to fly that day and using tranquilizers for your pets is not recommended. The change of altitude and pressure may cause more harm to your little friend.

Also, make sure you are traveling with the right pet carrier, especially if your dog or cat is not a service or emotional support animal. It has to fit completely under the seat in front of you for takeoff and landing. All airlines have different regulations regarding pets and pet carriers on board. Again, check with your airline regarding measurements and rules.

When traveling with Lulu to an international destination, you may need a health certificate and updated vaccinations. Every country has a different list of regulations regarding entering with pets. You would be very surprised at how incredibly strict some of these rules are. It is extremely important to check with the embassy of the country you are visiting for rules and regulations regarding pets. All this information can be found online.

Unfortunately, we see more and more ESAs onboard airplanes and other modes of transportation, even in stores and supermarkets. In all my years as a flight attendant I have never seen so many ESA cats and dogs as I have; they are on almost every single flight I work today. I had twelve emotional support animals on one single flight to Albany, New York one day. It was clear that some of those were not actual ESAs, but unfortunately it is illegal for me or other employees to challenge that, especially when they have notes from their doctors. Airlines are now trying to crack down on fake letters for ESAs or service dogs. These letters can be purchased from many online sites, sometimes for an extremely low cost. Fake service dog vests can get you inside the cabin with Lulu, but her behavior can give her away. Well-trained service dogs would not behave in any way other than they are trained to behave, especially when interacting with other pets. Even if it is hard to prove, claiming your animal is a service animal or an ESA is not right, and it may cause more restricted rules in the future regarding these animals and their owners.

One time a lady brought her pet on one of the flights I was working with one of my dear friends, with whom I had worked many times before. At boarding we noticed the woman had a pet inside her own carrier, but it was moving a lot for a small animal. I remember asking if it was a dog and she mentioned some breed I can't even spell. All I could see was a little face through the small holes on one of the sides of the carrier. She followed all the rules and placed the dog under the seat in front of her. The little dog was out of control, barking and moving intensely inside the carrier. We actually questioned whether we should take off like that, but we were late, and we decided to go, as the dog was secured inside its bag. All we could hear was growling and the bag was actually moving. For some reason, every time my coworker would pass by that row, the dog would bark. At one point, while doing our service, my friend passed by the little angel again, and I am not kidding you, the whole carrier came out into the aisle behind my friend's legs and followed her for nearly two rows. She was scared for a couple of seconds, but then we started to laugh. We could not believe it. That dog could make the whole carrier move.

Another time, after we told a gentleman and his partner to keep their cat inside of its bag, I was delivering drinks when I suddenly noticed a commotion way in the back, and some people were screaming. I dropped my drinks and I saw the other flight attendants trying to get something on the floor. That precious kitty escaped, and it was running all over the cabin. It was probably very afraid, as well. It was quite an experience, trying to catch this big cat that was jumping all over the place, even on top of people's seats. They learned their lesson that day. As embarrassing as it was for them, it was extremely comical trying to catch this animal at 36,000 feet. When bringing pet cats onboard, you have to be very considerate of others, especially those with allergies.

When you are traveling, and you are allergic to anything, including animals, it is very important to communicate that information to your airline at the time of booking or when you get to the airport, so they can accommodate you. Unfortunately, even if you have an allergy to dogs and there is a service dog next to you, by law we have to re seat you instead of the dog owner.

If you are traveling with a regular pet, a service dog or an emotional support animal, be respectful of others. There are also many rules and regulations protecting others. For example, if you have a service dog or ESA, you can keep them on your lap or the floor, but at no time can the animal touch the seat. Even if you buy an extra seat for Lulu, she cannot be seated next to you, for health reasons. Airlines can't clean the hair off of those seats between every flight. Many flight attendants and pet lovers may break the rules, so your pet friend can travel more comfortably, but do not argue with a crew member who is simply doing his or her job regarding by not allowing Lulu to sit on top of the seat or to be let out of her cage. Don't ever say that your flight attendant on your last flight let you do it. You just ruined it for you and everybody else.

If you decide to bring your special friend on board, you may need the assistance of the inflight crew at some point. Coming from Boston to Florida once, this young lady had a small and beautiful puppy with her. It was her first time bringing her dog on an airplane, so she was not only a little nervous, but she also had no idea what to do. The dog was adorable and did not bark or growl at any time. It was the perfect pet. At one point the lady came to the back and started talking to us about her new dog and how excited she was. Almost one hour before landing passengers started to come to the back acting very distressed before heading to the lavatories. I immediately heard the DING of the call button from the same area the adorable puppy and her owner were. As I got closer, I could smell a horrible stink coming from that location. It was bad. I remember one man saying, “I think the dog shit all over the place”.

As I got closer to the row, I couldn’t even breathe. It was horrible. The lady was trying to get up at the same time and she said, “Sorry; I have to take him to the bathroom”. I said ok and decided to take a look at her seat. OMG, it was like something just exploded on the floor! The smell was just horrendous, and people nearby were already moving to other seats. The lady came back, and I heard people calling her horrible names. They were starting to become very rude to the pet owner, but she didn’t know what to do. There was crap all over the place, really bad. As she started to cry and panic, I told her to relax; that we would help her.

I never thought in all my years of doing this job that I would be cleaning dog shit on an airplane, but I did. We brought everything we could to clean it up. I could still hear passengers saying horrible things to her, but it wasn’t her fault; it could have happened to anybody. After we landed they had to take the airplane out of service, which probably caused another unexpected delay. She was very thankful to the crew and actually wrote a very nice letter to the company. To this day, many of my coworkers call me the crap cleaner.

CHAPTER 12

SEX AND PORN

It may be very hard to believe, but some people really do try to have sex on airplanes, including in the lavatory. We all have some type of fantasy, including having sex in a pressurized metal tube flying at 37,000 feet at high speed, but I assure you it is not one of mine. Maybe after all the years working as a flight attendant and knowing how disgusting almost everything around us is and knowing there are so many germs. My bare ass would never touch the leather of a passenger seat or the walls inside the lavatory. Still, that does not stop some people from trying to join the famous Mile High Club. Many people have gotten arrested and banned from the airlines for this exact reason. If you have sex on my flight and you are so careful about it I can't even tell, good for you, but you have to be respectful of others around you, especially minors. It is still illegal to have sex in an airplane cabin or in the lavatories. Two adults are not allowed to enter an airplane lav unless it is for health reasons. If you are caught having sex on an airplane it may be the most expensive sex you ever have in your life. Depending on what country, airline or destination, the consequences may be severe, including a very large fine for all parties involved. If getting a blowjob on an airplane is so important to you that you are willing to risk completely ruining your vacation and your marriage when your husband or wife finds out, then you are a complete idiot. Often people are caught having sex on airplanes, and videos are shared online of passengers caught in the act. Some of them act like they don't have a care in the world.

Once I was on a very busy, nearly full flight in the middle of the day. I was returning from the back to my galley in the front of the aircraft. I decided to serve myself a cup of coffee and I noticed some passengers trying to get my attention in very weird way. The young lady by row 9 was signaling something or someone. I went to see what she needed. Others in the same area tried to get my attention as well. Everybody was pointing at the old man seated in 7 D, aisle seat. When I turned I could not believe my eyes. The guy was sitting comfortably, watching a very intense porn scene on a very large screen tablet. I was in shock. What do you do in these cases? I went over to his seat, got down to his level and told him to turn it off. Can you believe the guy just gave me a look and asked me why? I told him that could get him arrested, because it was illegal to view porn in plain sight of everyone around him, including the family with minors right behind him. I remember the father of the kids behind him telling him very in a very loud and upset voice, "Dude, turn that shit off."

He had his headset on, but it was very clear to those next to him and behind what he was watching. After a second warning he finally turned his tablet off. Listen, I am not an angel, and I would be lying to you if I told you I never watched porn before, but there is a place for that. Sitting in an aisle seat in the front of the airplane watching porn is not a very smart idea, especially with kids around. That can get you in trouble and it can be a huge embarrassment.

On your next flight if you still decide you want to join the Mile-High Club either with someone or by yourself, think about everything I just told you and decide whether it is worth it if you get caught. Still want to invite that lovely stranger you just met only minutes ago and take them on a lovely date to the lavatory? Always remember, LOCK YOUR DOORS.

If you don't lock your doors, you could wind up humiliated. On a flight to California in the middle of the night, we somehow failed to notice anybody going to one of the lavatories in the back, next to our galley. Night flights can get really boring, so we often pass the time by telling each other our life stories. Suddenly, one of our flight attendants went to use the restroom. The door was unlocked, and, to our great surprise, we saw two nearly naked women having the best time of their lives. I heard a couple of screams - not only from my co-worker, but from the women, as well. At least four or five rows of passengers woke up startled and wondering what was happening. It was so embarrassing for everyone involved. I am sure they learned their lesson and they never forgot to lock a public bathroom door again, unless of course it was meant as an invitation!

CHAPTER 13

FOOD AND DRINKS

Many domestic airlines here in the US or in other countries will offer what we call inflight service, some better than others. This may vary depending on what airline you take and also on the length of your flight. I remember many years ago airlines would serve you a full meal on a two- and a half hour flight between Miami and New York. Those times are gone, unless you pay a lot more to sit in premium seats, including first class. These days, many airlines will not offer any food on short flights, even in first class. Usually, on flights over four hours, you will see a better meal service.

When your airline does not offer food inflight or if you have dietary or religious restrictions, you are free to bring your own food. Almost all airlines will let you bring your own food onboard. However, this can also make you enemy number one inside the cabin, if you decide to eat your very delicious fermented herring accompanied by boiled eggs. Depending on what airline you are traveling with, they may ask you to stop. Use your common sense when bringing food onboard that will make your fellow passengers very jealous or totally throw up in disgust.

You can bring your own food from home and go through security or TSA with no problem, as long it's solid and contains no more than 3.4 oz of any liquid, gel, or even salad dressing. When bringing fruits or vegetables on international flights to the US, the Department of Agriculture will not let you bring any of that into the country, in case you don't finish it on the flight. It is very good idea to check with your airline or your country of departure with regard to what food items you can bring with you.

Now, I don't know about you, but when I travel I tend to bloat. My pants start to feel a little tight as the day goes on. Maybe it is all psychological or maybe it is true that we tend to bloat on an airplane due to all altitudes and pressure changes. I completely try to eliminate all carbonated drinks, including sodas. That will only make you feel even more bloated. The best option is to drink water.

I am also not a big fan of the hot water on airplanes, especially old airplanes. Have you asked your flight attendant for coffee before just to find out it tastes totally awful? It's the water. You can brew the best coffee on an airplane and the water will make it taste like something else. The same goes with tea. It is totally up to you. They say hot water kills everything, right?

I'm always amazed by the amount of food some people can consume on a two-hour flight. Just because it is free you shouldn't eat like the apocalypse is coming after your flight, or as though you are going into hibernation soon, just like a bear. It doesn't bother me or other flight attendants to give you your 5th snack with your four drinks; that's our job, at least when we are not that busy, but guess who is going to have to help you clean up when you get sick during turbulence? Me. Just think about it this way; when you are home watching some romantic movie on TV, do you go to the refrigerator and take out two sodas, a juice, and some water, then make some coffee, go to the pantry and grab five different snacks before taking all of that to your sofa? Probably not. So why you are doing it on the airplane? Is a free bag of potato chips worth getting sick? Travel smart, be smart.

As I mentioned in prior chapters, alcohol consumption on an airplane can totally go the other direction if you are not careful about how much you can handle. Drinking on an airplane, due to the altitude or pressure, can get you to the border line pretty fast. Some people can drink as much as they want and still manage to appear completely fine. There is actually not a written rule about how much you can drink on an airplane. Your crew will decide how much you can drink and when to stop. Coming onto a flight drunk is completely prohibited and you may be asked to step outside until you can tell me how many fingers I am holding in front of you.

Sometimes passengers are able to make it to their seats and it is not until later on in the flight that we realize they had way too much fun at the bar outside while waiting for the delayed flight. When this happens, your flight attendant can deny you any alcoholic beverage and completely cut you off. Arguing, screaming, or acting like a little child will only get you into more trouble. Just like in a bar, flight attendants have to be very careful how much alcohol you are consuming. This is one of the reasons it is totally illegal to serve your own alcohol while flying. At many airlines you can bring the bottle of champagne or vodka you bought at the terminal if you want to celebrate your new job or even your honeymoon. You cannot serve yourself or anybody around you without our consent, however. This may also vary depending on the airline, country or destination. Some airlines will not permit you to bring any alcoholic beverages to the cabin at all. Do not risk it. We will take that bottle and serve you ourselves. This way we know when to stop. You can bring little bottles of rum through the checkpoint, but you can't serve yourself inside the cabin. Also, alcohol is a good revenue income for airlines, although many airlines will serve you free alcohol on international flights. One of my favorite European airlines will always have free champagne for the whole cabin on international flights. Do not feel embarrassed by asking your flight attendant if alcohol is free or not. Usually, international and some domestic US airlines will have a magazine or menu in the seat bag pocket in front of you with detailed information about your options onboard.

Food choices also may vary depending on your destination and the airline you are taking. Almost all airlines will tell you on their website whether food will be served on your flight. Also, you may be able to select any special diet you may have. Usually those who request a special meal will be served first on the flight. Those of you who decide to buy your tickets using a third-party website may have the option to do so there even when the airline does not give the option. Always check directly with the airline.

Some international airlines will hire very well-known chefs for their culinary choices inside the cabin. Some may even offer a food menu in economy class. For first class passengers the experience is sometimes so extraordinary that you may even question whether you are actually on an airplane traveling that fast. On one of my vacation trips to Ireland, I swear the food I was served had to be from a secret ingredient. Until this day, I still don't know if it was beef or chicken. It was totally unknown not only to me, but to my friends as well.

One particular European airline doesn't offer the best service, but they have the most delicious pastries I ever had. They are simply delicious. If I fly with them again, it would be for the delicious dessert.

Never be afraid to ask the flight attendant for seconds. Remember that it is all in the way you ask. Always remember that being nice can take you far, and sometimes get you extra dessert.
If airplane food is not your thing, bring your own. Just avoid bringing fish!

Now, I am not being judgmental, but when we do snack service in the premium cabin, people tend to be more careful, especially if we are using a basket for the snacks. As soon as we pass that border right after row seven, however, it is like someone just threw a cow into the Amazon River and piranhas are trying to get their share before more piranhas arrive. Sometimes flight attendants nearly lose control of their baskets.

Most airlines have magazines or menus with a list of everything they offer onboard. At least take a look to see if you can find what you are looking for before asking, "What do you have?" After all, we usually offer the same thing, sodas, juices, coffee and tea. Do you know how annoying it is when you ask every passenger what they want, only to be asked the same question, over and over again?

CHAPTER 14

HYGIENE

I am not going to lie to you. There are millions of bacteria all around us when we travel, especially on anything we all touch; call buttons, armrests, window shades - everywhere. If you are a germ freak, then I recommend bringing your own anti-bacterial wipes or lotions. Use odor free products as much as you can so you don't disturb the person next to you with your eucalyptus mint lotion. Even though you and I may love eucalyptus, your fellow passengers may not. Unfortunately, people use those tray tables for all types of things, including changing baby diapers or even to rest their bare feet. Next time you want to put your sandwich or your crackers directly on top of that tray table, think again!

Walking around in your bare feet is something you should avoid when inside the cabin or visiting the lavatory. I always see people, including children, going to the lavatories with no shoes or socks. Maybe you don't care, or maybe you are germs' best friend, but to me, that is a very disgusting habit. Airlines really try their best to clean the interior, including carpets and lavatories, while the airplanes are resting overnight, but between flights it's a different story. There just isn't enough time to do a perfect job. Depending on where the aircraft is at that moment it may or may not get a good cleaning. They usually do a very superficial cleaning so that you, the customer, can't see the larger objects, but only once in a while will they do a good, antiseptic cleaning. I remember telling the cleaning crew in Costa Rica that we should bring every aircraft there at least once for a good cleaning. They cleaned everything. Every tray table was cleaned with an antibacterial spray and I even saw a woman cleaning the overhead bins. It was amazing. Whoever used that lavatory first probably had the cleanest ever. Amazing.

Now, think about everything that falls on the floor, day by day, including fluids from the girl who got sick on the previous flight or all of the nails from the guy clipping his toe nails behind you. Just leave your shoes on. If you are taking a long flight and want to be comfortable, leave your socks on. Whatever you do, be kind to the person in front of you and do not place your bare feet between the seats near their head, as I see once in a while. That's very disturbing. Nobody needs to see your unmanicured and smelly feet.

Finally, before you exit the plane, please pick up after yourself. Think about the time it takes for the cleaning crew to pick up and clean that incredibly dirty row you've left behind. In many cases your flight attendants are responsible for picking up after you. Isn't their pain enough after they have had to be attentive to your one hundred requests during the flight? Now, cleaning will take a little longer and boarding time for the next flight will be a little late, just because you decided to throw everything you ate during the flight onto the floor. Sometimes I wonder if we are transporting human beings or pigs from a farm, although I am almost certain that pigs wouldn't leave as much dirt behind. If you have too much trash with you, you can always ask for a trash bag from your inflight crew. The seat bag pockets are mostly for magazines, books, safety cards, and maybe your tablets. They are not for full cans of soda, your unfinished burger, or the very dirty diaper you are left with after you decide to change your baby on the floor. Use your common sense. Don't be that person.

CHAPTER 15

CONFRONTATION

I always tell my friends and family when they travel not to argue with the crew, either outside of the aircraft or inside. When you decide to start a fight with a flight attendant, even if you are 100% correct, there is a possibility you will lose the fight. Simply take their name and flight information and contact the airline after your finish your trip. Remember, there are many regulations while traveling on an airplane. When traveling inside a US carrier you may have to adhere to Federal Rules and Regulations mandated by the Government, especially the FAA, and creating a disturbance in the cabin will automatically become a federal disturbance. Trust me when I tell you it is not worth it.

We were going on vacation once to Las Vegas from South Florida and connecting in Charlotte. We decided to splurge a little since it was my 45th birthday, so we bought first class tickets. As an employee, I can basically can fly almost all airlines for free domestically, but I did not want to deal with the standby situation, especially to a popular destination. I was very excited, and we arrived at the airport early to check all our bags. We immediately went to the first-class cabin line and waited and waited. Nobody even looked at us. After a while an employee very rudely told us that we had to get into the main cabin line or check in at the kiosk. The whole experience was just horrible, but at that moment we had two options: start an argument with the employee about why he was so rude to us and take the chance that it might escalate to something bigger, or just leave it alone, take his name and report it to the airline after we came back. We decided to stay calm and quiet and let him guide us through the check-in process. We were not going to let this one person ruin our amazing vacation to Vegas.

Overall, we had a pretty good flight. All the flight attendants were actually very attentive and nice. On our way back, however, we were not so lucky; we had the flight attendant from hell. First class was pretty full, and we were never offered anything to drink. She was too busy texting. The way she talked to the passengers was awful and very disrespectful, too; We couldn't believe her attitude. At that moment I realized there was nothing we could do except sit there quietly and take it. As a flight attendant myself it is always very uncomfortable to have this type of encounter with other colleagues. Engaging in an argument with Evolina from hell would be a total waste of time, and I would probably end up getting arrested.

Flying can be so much easier when you respect others. For some reason, many people feel entitled to things these days. When you travel you do deserve the best service, especially after paying a lot of money for your trip, but that does not make you the Sultan of the flight. Airlines employees are not your slaves or personal servers. They have to work with the other two hundred passengers on your flight. Now, I'm going to give you some advice which I will repeat throughout the book, because I want to make sure you remember it when you are done reading: smiling and being polite can take you far.

I was flying from Havana, Cuba on an Airbus once, and the flight was actually extremely open. For some reason, in Havana they assign peoples' seats right there at the airport; passengers don't have the choice of choosing for themselves. Havana rules, I guess. Anyway, a family with two infants came on board and immediately sat in the emergency exit row. As you remember, there are rules about sitting in those seats. One of those rules is that only people over fifteen years old can occupy an emergency exit seat. After explaining to them what the procedure was, they apologized and waited for instructions. The entire row behind was completely empty and after asking them if it was ok for them to sit there, instead, they all very nicely agreed. Each passenger could have actually had their own row on that flight.

Boarding continued very slowly, and two gentlemen arrived. One was short, in his mid-fifties, with a nice gray guayabera and very strong cologne we could all smell throughout the aircraft. He proceeded to his seat - the same seat I just gave to the family with the babies. I could see hands flying around so I decided to go see what was going on since I was the only Spanish speaker on the flight. I apologized to him and told him the reason I had to make the changes. I even offered him the seat right behind that one, which was totally empty. He started arguing that was his seat, and that he was not moving from there. I even offered him a better upgraded seat up front, just to avoid more arguing. Nope, he would not move. I never saw anybody so stubborn in my life. Everything would have been great if only he didn't star cursing and screaming at the family, using very bad language in both English and Spanish. Earlier, he had told the other flight attendant he only spoke Spanish. He was being very loud, and another coworker decided to intervene to help out. Suddenly, he pushed the flight attendant, so I had to place myself between him and her. He never touched me or called me any names. He was only being disrespectful toward women. I told the other crew member to call the authorities and I told the passenger that pushing, arguing or offending an inflight crew was a federal crime and that he could be fined for that, but he didn't care. At that point, Cuban authorities came on board and took him away.

Now, I have a lot of patience, especially with disruptive passengers, and I will give them many chances before I decide to kick them off a flight. However, touching or disrespecting another of my crew, especially if they are women and you are a man, will get you a first-class ticket to the local county jail.

Another rule that must be obeyed on all airlines in the US and on the majority of international airlines is that smoking and the use of electronic devices are prohibited during the flight. There is zero tolerance for people trying to smoke in the cabin or use electronic cigarettes (vaping). Cigarettes can cause fires and trust me; you don't want a fire at 36,000 feet in the middle of nowhere. Vaping and electronic cigarettes are also banned from many flights. First of all, vaping is rude. As much as you may love to vape, the people around you may feel differently. If you really have to do it on a 12-hour flight, then be smart and use the lavs, away from the smoke detectors. By no means am I telling you to do this or giving you permission, as this is completely illegal, and a flight attendant will tell you to stop. E-cigarettes are powered by lithium batteries, which can self-ignite if damaged or exposed to severe external effects, like temperature or cabin pressure, mostly because of manufacturing defects. This is the main reason you should not put your e-cigarette inside your checked bag. Bring it with you, but make sure it is completely off.

I had a huge fight on a flight once because someone decided to use an e-cigarette and the man sitting next to her said he was allergic to it. I am not a doctor, so I don't even know if that was true or not, but she knew she could not do it and her neighbor had the right to make it stop. By the time the crew went over there, the man had already received a couple of slaps to his face and several insults. My fellow coworkers even had some very nice scratches to remember the incident for weeks. We had to pull her out of her seat and take her to an empty row. She was very disruptive, and we had no choice but to make an unplanned landing at the closest airport to drop her off. All this drama just for an e-cigarette. It's clear that some people simply love to argue about everything. No matter how good the service is or if you treat them like kings and queens, they will find a reason to argue with you, sometimes about very incredible things.

Overhead bin space is the cause of many of these types of arguments between passengers and crew on some destination flights. On some flights you will never hear anybody argue about any of this nonsense, while on other flights, it seems like everybody is mad at the world. As I've said before, overhead bin space is shared space. That means it's for everyone to share. Sometimes flights are full, and we run out of space, mainly because others did not follow the instructions we repletely mention during the whole boarding process. Over and over they are told to put only one bag on top and the smaller one under the seat, but they just don't care about the person right behind them. Sometimes it truly feels like we are talking to a wall. Others think they are the only ones on the flight and put their little rollaboard right in the middle, taking over the whole space. When someone comes to accommodate their own bags, just moving the bag that is blocking the whole space starts an argument. I love it when they say, "Hey, don't touch my bag", to the passenger or even to the crew. Once, when one man said that to me, I responded, "How about I touch whatever I feel like up here? If you don't want your bag to be touched, then put it in correctly". Before starting a bag-fight, always ask a flight attendant for help. They may find you another space. Just be nice.

Seat selection is another reason for so many fights and arguments inside the cabin. The majority of airlines have assigned seats, and they are called "assigned" for a reason. If your boarding pass says 17E, look for that seat. There is no reason why you should be seated in 4A during boarding, especially when half of the plane is still outside. If you come aboard and encounter that situation, very nicely ask that person to doublecheck to see if that is their actual seat. If that does not help you solve the problem, call for a crew member to help you. Flight attendants or even ground crew will find a solution for the mistake. Confronting the customer seated in your seat with foul language or even aggressiveness will only get you kicked off that flight. Now, I love the City of New York; in fact, I used to live near Forest Hills a long time ago, but I must admit that passengers traveling to and from the Big Apple can be a little aggressive and demanding, especially when it comes to this topic.

People travel for many reasons and sometimes they do so during very tough times in their lives. Maybe you just got served with divorce papers or you lost a family member. Whatever the reason is, you have no right to treat others in a bad way, especially people you don't know and who may spend the next five to 17 hours seated next to you in a very confined space. Take a sedative, do some yoga, have a drink, or whatever it takes for your body to relax. Taking your problems out on others will just make it worse. Try to communicate with others in a kindly manner. Sometimes your inflight crew will help you feel better if only you ask. Confronting others and starting arguments or fights inside a metal tube is not something that you want or need to see later on some website that will only make you feel regretful and stupid. You can search for and watch hundreds of airplane fights on the internet, some of them occurring for practically no reason at all.

It's not difficult to avoid confrontation. Lately, more and more people seem to think it is ok to start a fight on a flight for some ridiculous reason. Respect others like you want others to respect you. Treat your neighbor like you want to be treated. It is actually that simple. Leave your anger and frustration outside in the terminal. Read a book, watch a tv show or a movie, or even meditate. I travel a lot for pleasure and I have encountered many confrontational people, including crew members. I have a choice between going down to their level or simply ignoring them. If you are having a problem with someone, ask others for help or find another solution. Aggressiveness is never the answer and avoiding confrontation will make your trip more pleasurable. Sometimes you may even get upgraded when you seek for help.

CHAPTER 16

COMMON SENSE

Having a little common sense when we travel can make our life much easier. Think before you react and think before you ask questions or do something you may regret later. Every time I go to the airport I always try to figure out why some people act the way they do.

For example, have you ever seen a person coming into a terminal using the automatic entrance doors with a cart full of bags, who then decides to stop as soon as they get inside, blocking everyone behind them? What about that person using the escalators at the airport who blocks everyone behind him because he or she just decided to stop immediately at the top or bottom?

Now, the airline I work for has live tv, that clearly uses a satellite signal. I can't tell you how many people on the airplane ask questions like: "Is the cable on?" or "Do you have cable?' Unfortunately, if he used cable, there would have to be a very long cable hanging behind the aircraft!

When coming to the airport, you may have to go through the security checkpoint. You will need to pass through a metal detector to check for metal objects you may have on you. If you are one of those people who likes to wear tons of metal, including bracelets and chains, you may get an extra security search, or you may have to take extra time to take off all that metal of before passing through. You never really know what will set it off. You can bring some metal objects with you – a ring or perhaps a bracelet - and the alarm will not even beep. My watch will go off sometimes, but not always. Maybe it depends on how the machine is set up. A word of advice: if you have a medical implant, it is very smart to let the officer know so they can give you a "pat down" and not put your health at risk. The same goes for heart monitors. Now, if you travel with ten pounds of metal, including your beautiful silver neck choker, you may set off the alarm. Don't be mad; it's part of the TSA's job and it's the whole reason those machines are there in the first place. If you want to wear all your jewelry at the same time on that trip, put it on after you pass the security checkpoint.

One time I was waiting at the gate for my working international flight. Usually the agents will give me all the paperwork I need for the flight. As I was waiting, a gentleman came to the podium after his name was called to check for his passport information.

"May I see your passport, please?" the agent asked very nicely.

"What?" He responded.

She asked the same question again, even a little slower this time.

"What passport?" he said. "I don't have one."

We all looked at each other at the same time with confusion. Why didn't he have a passport when he was traveling to an international destination from the US? Had he been living under a rock for the past thirty years? His facial expression remained the same; blank. I am almost certain that his mind was traveling far away from the airport; maybe in another galaxy. The agent had to call a supervisor to explain to him that he could not travel without a passport to another country from the United States. As I entered the aircraft to get ready for my flight, he was still arguing with the airline representative about not having a passport.

This is why it is so important to check the rules with regard to your destination, so you will have everything you need, and this won't happen to you. If you are traveling from the United States to an international destination, you may need a passport to travel, unless it is a US territory. Even if you travel within the Schengen Area, officials may reinstate border control without notice. Use common sense; use your passport or proof of nationality when doing so. Oh, and make sure your passport does not expire in a few days.

One lady in particular was terrified when she arrived at the gate and saw another flight's information on the tv monitor. She became upset when her flight information was not displayed on the monitor. Was the airline playing a trick on her? The gate agent asked for her boarding pass and started to laugh; her flight was almost five hours later, and she was extremely early. Still, she asked why her flight was not on the tv. The agent very cordially told her:

"Ma'am, there are other flights leaving at this same gate before yours; probably like four or five". Keep checking."

On another occasion, the weather outside was just horrible. The wind was so strong you could hear it whistling through the doors. It was only noon, but between the dark clouds and the heavy rain, you might have thought it was a night flight to Austin, Texas. The airport was very crowded due to the many delays of all the airlines at that terminal. When an announcement was made that the airport was being closed because of the thunder and for the safety of their ramp employees, one gentleman became extremely upset. He approached the gate and demanded to know why his flight was delayed. For a moment I thought I was part of that scene from The Devil wears Prada, when a woman is demanding her jet be sent in a hurricane, but this was for real; he wanted answers, right away. The agent told him that the weather was the cause of the delay, but that was not enough for him and he demanded to speak to a supervisor. The whole crew was already there waiting for our airplane to arrive, which was probably flying around waiting for an opportunity to land. Then the captain pointed to the big glass window and said to him;

"See? Do you see that big storm right outside that window? There is your answer. We can't fly like that. Got it?" The man had nothing else to say, except, "Ok, ok, I got it." Then he returned very calmly to his family.

Working for an airline, I can understand why some people may say that common sense is uncommon. When the captain is telling everyone in the cabin that it will be very bumpy for the next five minutes and you even see the flight attendants taking their seats for their own security, do you really think that is the perfect time to use the lavatory or to ask for a coffee or a hot tea? Sure, I'm going to pour and bring you a hot tea right then, and you can go to the lavatory, too. Just remember; when that big airplane traveling at 500 miles an hour starts to shake with you inside the bathroom, it is not going to be pleasant. Really; stay seated and respect the signs. If you see the flight attendants taking their seats, do so as well.

Evacuating an airplane is one thing we all hope we never have to do, especially because of a fire. Things can go very wrong in just a few seconds. Depending on the airline or country you may hear different evacuation commands from the cabin crew. When an evacuation occurs, there is no time for anything. Just exit as fast as you can and try to help others. When watching several videos online of evacuations of different carriers around the world, I was very surprised to see people taking their luggage with them. One of the rules of an emergency evacuation is not to take anything with you.

Your life is your priority as well as the life of your fellow passengers. You have no right to block them from escaping quickly simply because you need to take your Louis Vuitton bag out of the overhead compartment. Those seconds you waste can be the difference between life and death. Of course, at that moment we will all know whether your bag is fake or genuine; I know some of you would never leave your genuine Louis behind! Use your common sense.

Another time I was visiting a little town in Colombia called Manizales, and I was waiting with my travel partner at the gate area for our flight. It was a very spacious waiting area for departures to national destinations inside Colombia. Some of those flights do not have a jet bridge, and a bus has to take you to the aircraft which is parked in a remote location. Suddenly the airline representative made a pre-boarding announcement:

"Ladies and gentlemen, in just a few minutes we will be ready to board the bus for those of you flying to Manizales."

A lady around my age got up and went over to the agent at the gate. She was extremely upset, and she asked in a very loud voice,

"What do you mean a bus? I paid a lot of money to go to Manizales on an airplane, and you are telling me we are taking a bus? This is ridiculous."

I couldn't hear the answer she received since nearly everybody in earshot started to laugh uncontrollably, including us. That was the perfect example of someone who not only paid no attention to announcements, but had no common sense, either, since she was clearly at the airport - not at a bus station.

Sometimes these situations are funny, and have no consequences, but other times they are not funny at all. My intention in telling these stories is not to make fun of anybody. It's just that encountering these types of people can be very annoying - especially when you are in a rush.

For example, have you ever tried to take an escalator at the airport and you encounter a lovely couple trying to use the electric escalator with two babies and a double stroller? I have, and they always take forever before trying to figure out how to do it. We are all left waiting there until they give up and finally decide to take the stairs. Such people have no common sense at all. Such situations are what elevators are for. In addition, they have completely ignored all the signs that warn against bringing strollers on the escalator.

You would hope that once people had children they would gain a little common sense, but that's not always the case, and other people often have to pay the price for it. One of my favorite anonymous quotes about common sense is: "Common sense is not a gift; it's a punishment. You have to deal with everyone who doesn't have it." For instance, I see many parents traveling with their kids every day. Some kids are angels and won't even move the whole flight. I have no idea how their parents do it, but these children will not even cry at all for hours. With others, it's a different story, however. I have had families with kids who act as though they are at an amusement park, jumping in their seats, playing with the tray tables of everybody around them, and so on. I can't tell you how many times I have been taking their orders when the parents ask, "Can we have two coffees with cream and sugar, two apple juices, four waters and a hot tea?" They should know better. Coffee and hot tea does not mix with jumping kids or infants. That is just an accident waiting to happen. Where is their common sense when asking for hot drinks around their unruly children, when it is obvious someone will get hurt?

Passengers need to use common sense when using lavatories too. We all have no choice but to share the same lavatory. When you need to use one, CLOSE THE DOOR! There is a little lock inside for you to do exactly that. Guess what may happen when you do not close that door? Someone may come in and encounter a situation that is unpleasant, not only for you, but also for the passenger that has been subjected to the sight of your naked body. It is very embarrassing for both people involved. You can avoid embarrassment simply by closing and locking the door behind you.

Even when getting to land, people forget to exercise their common sense. For example, on one flight I was on some time back, we were getting ready to land, and as we were approaching the ground, probably at 900 feet, one lady got up, opened the overhead bin compartment, took out her rollaboard and started walking toward the front. We were landing, for God's sake. Where did she think she was going? One of my coworkers told her to sit down in a firm voice. She stood there for couple of seconds, looked around and took her seat again. Unbelievable.

According to Merriam-Webster, common sense is defined as *sound and prudent judgement based on a simple perception of the situation or fact*. Others have said it is *the ability to think and behave in a reasonable way and to make good decisions*. Whatever the meaning of common sense is according to the experts, I am very sure many out there have a lack of it. I swear some people have none; zero. I've even known some very well-educated people who graduated at the top of their class that have no common sense. The other day I witnessed someone at the airport behaving very stupidly toward a law enforcement officer, and I began to wonder whether people's behavior can be proved scientifically, to determine whether, as they get close to an airport, an invisible magnetic field interferes with their brain neurons. I am, of course, kidding, but it really does seem like that sometimes.

People often have no common sense when it comes to their stomachs. To save cost or for lack of time, many airlines no longer offer meal or drink service on short flights. One passenger became very upset because we had no breakfast available for him on a very short fifteen-minute flight from San Juan to Saint Thomas. I thought he was joking at first when he asked, so I responded in a joking manner. However, he was not kidding, and he wanted breakfast. We spent more time arguing about breakfast than the actual flying time to Saint Thomas. He even accused me of not serving him because I was lazy. He claimed that he was given breakfast last time he flew. What can you do when you encounter people like this? Unfortunately, there is nothing we can do except smile and continue with our lives. In my case, I also committed these stories to memory so that I could write this book for you.

There is one particular question I get during a flight, often in the middle of a very busy drink service. Someone will press the call button, so I immediately stop what I am doing to see what he needs. He is seated at the window seat very anxiously looking outside, and before you can even ask what they need, he will say something like,

"Do you know the name of that little piece of land we are flying over now?"

I always respond with, "Sorry, my GPS is off right now, but you can check the map on your tv." Hopefully they are flying on an airline with TVs or even a map channel at the time...

Health issues are another area for concern on airplanes. Many people have health or medical conditions that prevent them from traveling on an airplane. However, others need only to bring their medication with them and the problem is solved. If you need medication, you should keep it with you at all times. Putting it inside the bag you checked at the ticket counter or outside at the gate will not help you at all. Although we do have a whole supply of medical equipment onboard, your high blood pressure medication may not be available. Pack smart.

A while ago, there was a dad traveling along with his twins. They were beautiful kids; I remember mentioning that they should be models for a baby magazine. They were probably three or four years old. Now, at that point in time we had many snacks that contained peanuts or other nuts. As I was distributing snacks, he asked me not to serve anything with nuts as his kids were allergic to all nut products and they could get sick even breathing them in. I stopped completely, and I am very sure he could see the frustration in my face as I asked,

"You are telling me now? In the middle of the flight?"

I couldn't believe he chose to advise me about his kids' allergies in the middle of service at 3600 feet. I stopped distributing the nuts and I made an announcement about the allergy on board. His kids were fine, in the end., but these days there are different procedures regarding allergies on the airplane. Some airlines won't even serve nut products anymore, just to avoid lawsuits. Just to be sure, though, and for you own safety, make sure you mention any allergies when you make your reservation or when you get to the airport. It is public transportation; we can only do so much to avoid any complications.

On the other hand, if you are allergic to cats or dogs, there is a very high possibility you may have one of those travel companions under a seat near you. Tell your airline ahead of time so they can accommodate you. And no; opening a window to get fresh air isn't a solution. Believe it or not, however, I have actually had customers asking whether I can open a window in the cabin.

Foolish questions don't end there, though. I had a man once bring me a barf bag full of his own urine, asking what he was supposed to do with it. Stupidity at its best. Finally, if the flight attendant won't give something to you or it is not in front of you on your tray table, there is a possibility it doesn't belong to you. Do not go to the galleys and take food or anything else that is not intended for your enjoyment. If I leave my chicken sandwich with my dark chocolate Hershey bar I just bought at the airport before the flight on top of the counter, please do not take it. It may be the only food I will have the whole day. It is just not yours. Use your common sense.

CHAPTER 17

NON-REVS

For those of you who have no clue what non-revving is, I would be more than happy to clear that up for you. Almost all airlines will give their employees some type of flight benefits for them and their families. They can fly their own airline for free or for a small charge on standby status, and so can their spouses, parents and children. I am one of the lucky ones who has a company that will let me fly for free domestically or international; not only on my own airline, but on others as well, for a small fee plus taxes.

Those of you who work in this industry also know there are many rules and regulations regarding non-revs, depending on your airline or the airline you are traveling with.
Always check the rules that apply to the specific airline you will be taking.

I learned this lesson firsthand some time ago. I was ready to leave for my flight to Hawaii on another airline and I decided to stay in my uniform for the trip because it was easier and faster. Imagine my surprise when a representative of the airline informed me I could not go in uniform, and I had to change. I failed to check their rules and regulations regarding the proper way to non-rev with them. It's a good thing I had my bag with me, so I could change into casual business attire for the flight as required by that airline. Therefore, for those of you who work in the airline business, it is very important to double check their dress code before your flight.

Upgrades are another perk that employees may enjoy. We were traveling back from Madrid Barajas Airport one time, taking advantage of our benefits, and while we weren't upgraded to first class, we felt as though we had been. The crew was unbelievable. Other passengers around us started to look in our direction, and they were probably wondering who the hell we were. Maybe we were superstars from a Spanish soap opera or a famous singer from Spain. Champagne was flowing like a river, as well as their very delicious first-class desserts. We were in heaven. Now, don't be jealous! I can almost see your sad face. You might work at Disneyworld, for example, and receive free passes and many discounts I can only dream of. See?

Dress codes are extremely important for those who are non-revving, since they are representing their employer and they have to go by the rules of those letting them use their service. If you know jeans are forbidden in first class, then there is almost no chance they will let you upgrade to first class while non-revving.

Hundreds of airline employees have been left behind simply because they didn't follow the dress code of the airline they were taking.

Non-revving can be unpredictable, however. You may not actually make that flight, so those of us who non-rev from time to time know it is very important to have a Plan B, C, and sometimes D when traveling on standby. You must follow the same rules as regular passengers and perhaps even more. Give yourself plenty of time depending which airport you are leaving from. It may be your home airport and you are taking advantage of that wonderful KCM or Known Crewmember access, but anything can happen. Rules regarding KCM change periodically, so make sure you are updated with all information you may need.

Be smart and use your common sense when traveling on standby on any airline, depending on the time of the year. Flights to Europe from the USA during the summer months are very busy, and sometimes the airlines will block some days for non-rev flying. It also depends on the day of the week; traveling non-rev during the week can sometimes be a little easier than on weekends. It is very important to check the holidays or special events of the country or city you are visiting. If you are planning to visit the annual Albuquerque International Balloon Fiesta in October, you know that trying to go on standby on any airline that flies that route will be almost impossible.

There are many apps and social media help available these days for non-revving on different airlines. Employees of any airlines around the world are connected through social media to help those who seek help, including flight loads, dress code, or just to ask what the best time is to fly. Taking advantage of these options may be the difference between getting to your destination or not.

Remember; when you are non-revving you are taking advantage of your company's flying benefits. You must follow the rules and etiquette while flying under this benefit. It is very nice when we get upgraded to business class or first class by the crew. However, some airlines are not even allowed to do this for their own employees, so even if you bring them ten bags of candy as a gift, they still won't do it. Please do not expect it. Be polite and thankful, and don't be loud. Sometimes we take advantage of the alcoholic beverages they offer during a flight, but don't be silly; act accordingly. Don't expect anything for free, depending on the airline. If you are consuming something for sale, have your payment ready. Do not shout out to the world that you are non-revving. If someone asks, then you may tell them, but be discreet. A simple smile can take you far.

To illustrate this, a while ago we had a huge argument with a passenger. He didn't want to be told what he did, so he ignored rules and etiquette, from refusing to fasten his seatbelt to being extremely rude to the flight attendants. One by one we tried to talk to him about his behavior on the flight, but he remained a pain in the ass. After a small discussion with the cabin crew about staying seated for landing, he decided to call my fellow crewmember a bitch.

Ouch. You know there was going to be someone waiting for him at the front door to talk to him about his behavior. We were surprised to find out that he was flying for free as the family member of another employee. That was bad news for the poor employee who could have their benefits terminated just because this asshole didn't know how to behave inside an airplane. Unfortunately, it is to be expected that regular customers sometimes behave badly when they fly; after all, flying can be stressful and we all react differently to such situations, but we never expect to see that type of behavior from another employee or their family.

So, if you are non-revving and you make it to the flight, sit back, relax and enjoy it. If you are not an airline employee, then please let them have their fun.

CHAPTER 18

PREPARING FOR LANDING

Congratulations. You've made it through the flight and the inflight crew or the captain has just announced, "Ladies and gentlemen, we are one hundred and twenty miles from the airport. We will start our initial descent in just a few moments. Thank you for flying with us." As soon as you hear that, you have a decision to make. Should you stay seated and enjoy the rest of the flight or should you use the lavatory before they turn the seatbelt lights on? Easy decision, right?

First of all, I can assure you half of the people paid no attention to the announcement, and the other half will wait until the very end to decide. If you didn't use the restroom earlier and you think you may need to do so before landing, now is your opportunity. You still have couple of more minutes to get up, stretch your legs, and even put all your personal belongings back in the overhead. Just do not stress over it. It's an easy task.

This is also the time the cabin crew will be going around collecting anything you do not want anymore. Why wait until the last minute? Give it to them now.

Next, the seatbelt sign will go on and the inflight crew will make an announcement to all passengers on board that may sound like this: "Ladies and gentlemen, we started our initial descent and the Captain has turned on the seatbelt sign., Please return to your seats for landing."

At that moment, everyone suddenly wants to get up, whether to use the lavatories or for any other reason. You would think that the cabin crew had just told everyone to get up and do whatever they wanted, all the same time. It may be psychological; I don't know, I am not a psychologist, but there has to be a reason for this behavior, because it happens all the time. Sometimes I feel like I am talking to dead people. They don't even respond or acknowledge that we are talking to them.

This also seems to be the time when all babies suddenly need to be changed and people with disabilities want help to use the lavatories, as well. Your crew is probably busy preparing the galleys, cleaning up for the next flight, and just making sure everything is secure for landing. At ten minutes before landing there is still a long line waiting for the lavatories after a four-hour flight. Try to use the lavatories earlier on in your flight to avoid this problem.

At about ten thousand feet we need to prepare the cabin for landing. FAA regulations in the US requires all cabin crew to be ready for landing and to make sure everything is secured. The cabin crew will pass by one last time to make sure everything is secured, that tray tables and seatbacks are upright, that all laptops are off and stowed away, and that all bags are completely under the seat in front of you. This is the time I often feel like I am talking to kindergarten children. Come on; you know the rules. You know what you have to do. I am sure most of you have already done this before, so why wait for your flight attendant to tell you ten times before you actually comply? These are federal regulations, and in the end, you will have to comply anyway, so just do it.

This is also a very critical part of the flight. We are flying at a very low altitude and we may encounter some turbulence because of the clouds or the winds. It is just not safe to be up and walking around. Yet, believe it or not, some people choose this time to get up to use the restroom. If they only knew how unsafe this was, they wouldn't do it. Airlines receive thousands of complaints about flight attendants telling passengers to comply with the rules. Many years ago, I visited one of our call centers, and it was actually funny to hear these complaints directly. Some customers complain about everything, and they will sometimes demand free flights or miles on their accounts.

"The stewardess told me very rudely to put my seatbelts on."

"She told me to stow my laptop and I was still sending emails."

"I wanted to get out first, but he made me put my bag back in the overhead."

Now, I am not by any means suggesting that we are all angels or that we communicate these rules kindly to passengers at all times, but when we have to repeat ourselves several times to the same person, again and again, our patience may have a limit. For instance, the tone of our voice may change a little the seventh time we tell Mr. Smith to put the tray table in an up and locked position.

This is also not the time to bring your bags down and leave them in the middle of the aisle. If something happens during landing and we have to evacuate and run, guess what would happen with all of those bags blocking the exits? It's dangerous, so please don't do it.

Many airlines, including international carriers, lock the lavatories at this time, to ensure that nobody is inside when the plane lands. I can't tell you how many people have landed inside a bathroom, but I can tell you that it is not a pleasant experience.

Now, we all know some of you can't wait to get off the plane, but the air pressure in the cabin will not let you open any doors, including the emergency exit doors. Of course, this doesn't stop some crazies from trying to open them.

One time a young lady, probably in her early twenties, proceeded to the front of the cabin right before landing and tried to open the main entrance door, screaming at the top of her lungs that someone was trying to kill her. Maybe someone was, but I can assure you it wasn't anyone on that airplane! The crew had to restrain her and keep her under guard until we landed, and the medics and police arrived.

In another incident that made the news, another lady got up right before landing and started screaming uncontrollably: "Get me the f…. out of here!" while walking through the main aisle.

There was also an incident during a flight from New Jersey to Florida that I will never forget. I was serving the back of the cabin when a very well-dressed gentleman from South America started talking to me. He was telling me all kinds of stories about how he started his business and how well he did back in his country. He was so nice that I actually offered him some white wine and he accepted and continued to talk. Now, I only remember giving him only one drink, but after a while he fell completely asleep. He was seated on the aisle seat, on the right side of the aircraft, two rows before the last. During landing I heard his seatbelt click, so, from my jump seat, I told him to stay seated for landing. He totally ignored me and, just like he was at home in the privacy of his own bathroom, he dropped his zipper down and started to urinate all over the place. He was moving side to side while urinating, so everything and everyone who was nearby got wet. There were loud screams and people started to panic and move towards the windows and my galley. We actually touched down with passengers everywhere. I couldn't believe that the same guy who had been talking to me so calmly about his life was doing such a thing. After we got to the gate, airline supervisors accompanied by the police took him away.

While not as bad as urinating on an airplane, changing into a bathing suit right at your seat is also not wise. It's especially not a good idea to take off your jeans and underwear and replace them with your new Hawaiian-style shorts. That stunt probably got one man on my flight a little talking to by Mexican officers when we arrived, and probably a delay for the beach.

Touching down is actually one of my favorite parts of the flight; the ordeal is almost over, and we are safely on the ground. Many people will applaud as though they were at the theater and a play has just finished. Sometimes I feel like getting up, standing in the middle of the aisle, and saying, "THANK YOU! THANK YOU VERY MUCH!" No one knows why some people do this. Some say it is a cultural thing, depending on where you are flying to, but I still find it odd to hear applause at landing. After that, you hear all the seatbelts unbuckle at the same time, just like a song, throughout the whole cabin. This is when evil thoughts come out to play, and I wish the pilots would make a sudden, almost violent stop so we could see who ignored the announcement about keeping their seatbelts on until we get to the gate.

Just stay seated until we arrive at the gate; it's as simple as that. There are very good reasons why there are rules about not getting up while the plane is taxiing on the runway. You may get hurt or you may hurt someone else. Even if you decide to get up, there is no place to go yet. The doors will stay closed until we get to the gate.

CHAPTER 19

GETTING OFF THE AIRPLANE

During those final seconds while the aircraft is arriving at the gate the internal countdown starts. You can almost hear the engines start to get ready for the race. Deplaning can be almost magical. When an old man, who came on board in a wheelchair and couldn't even walk to his seat, suddenly gets up and practically runs to the front of the cabin to get out first, it's almost a religious experience.

At the first moment the plane stops, before the seatbelt sign is even turned off, everybody gets up at the same time. Everyone tries to get their luggage out of the bins without being careful of the faces they might break if they get hit by a huge rollaboard.

It actually takes couple of minutes for the ground crew to open the door, so just relax. I understand you have to catch a connecting flight that leaves in 15 minutes, but if you have no other plane to catch, then turn your engines off. This is the time when a wonderful flight can go to hell. People tend to argue a lot during disembarking - or deplaning, as we say in the US. And of course, that person who decided to go to the lavatory right after the seatbelt sign went off is now trying to make his way back to his seat when everyone else is up.

If you have a very tight connection, inform your flight attendant about it during the flight. We can actually accommodate you to a seat closest to the exit. Perhaps if you were nice and behaved yourself during the flight I will make everyone stay seated for just a couple of seconds, so you can make your way to the front. This usually works great, depending on the crowd, but they will only give you couple of seconds before they start rushing toward the doors, too, so be ready to run.

If you are traveling with a baby in a stroller; what is your rush to get off? You only have to wait for the ground crew to bring your stroller up anyway, and that may take a couple of more minutes. Blocking everyone else with all your baby gear and car seat will not make it come up any faster. Just relax, wait in your seats and let others pass.

Wheelchair passengers are my favorites, however. No matter how many times you tell these passengers to wait, they just won't. They always want to be the first ones to get out. Suddenly they find the energy and strength they didn't have when they came on board. I have actually seen wheelchair passengers run, leaving their wheelchairs behind. Alleluia!!! Another miracle flight. We seem to be able to cure people on board the plane.

My aunt is like that. When she flew out to visit she went everywhere with us during her stay. We even walked almost the whole of Miami Beach one day. When we went back to the airport, and while I was getting all her stuff out of the car, I noticed she was seated in a wheelchair and there was a man standing by ready to push her. I got worried for a moment and asked her if she was ok. With a big smile on her face she responded,

"Oh, yeah; I'm fine. This way I don't have to stand on line and I can board first".

I felt like I wanted to die. I couldn't believe a member of my own family was trying to cheat the system, but I didn't want to get into an argument right there. I'm sure that as soon as she arrived, she was the first one off of that plane.

Maybe some people are in a rush because they can't wait to get up and stretch their legs. That's understandable, but if you are in the back of the cabin, you probably have a couple of minutes before you can even move. Why do you feel the need to get up and retrieve your bags the moment the plane arrives at the gate? There is no way you can make it to the front, especially with that big rollaboard you are carrying. Why stand there like a fool, bending over very uncomfortably because the overhead bins prevent you from standing up straight? Stay in your seat, comfortably, until the people in the row in front of you start to move. Then it's your turn.

People try to cheat the system with their luggage, too. One of my pet peeves is when passengers come on board, leave their luggage at one of the overhead bins up front, and proceed to their seats all the way to the back of the airplane. Sometimes when I see that, I make them take their bags with them. It is just not fair for the passenger who is looking for space up front. Imagine traveling to airports like Punta Cana, Dominican Republic or Long Beach, California. Those airports allow passengers to exit the airplane from both the front and the back of the cabin. That's the only time I'll let those trying to be smart put their bags up front. It gives me so much pleasure seeing their faces when they find out they would have been the first ones to go, but now they have to wait to get their bags from the front. Cheat the cheater.

I also love it when people get upset at the passenger standing behind them with their bags, when they are doing exactly the same to the passenger right in front of them. Airlines have tried different methods to make exiting the airplane a little less stressful for passengers, but nothing works; it's human nature. Airlines that have less luggage in the cabins tend to do a faster turnaround of their aircrafts. The more they charge for luggage, the more they will see people bringing them on board. On the other hand, airlines that offer free checked luggage or that charge a fee for the luggage passengers bring onboard have better results when deplaning. It's common sense. Also, you get what you pay for. If you spend your money or miles on a first-class seat, you probably will be one of the first to exit. It is a lovely feeling. If you were lucky enough to buy an economy seat close to the doors as well, you are in luck. Many business people or connectors will pay extra to sit in those premium economy seats close to the exits, so they can leave first. In any case, we can make this experience a little less stressful. Just wait your turn; keep playing your video game or spend the time gathering your items so you are ready to go when it's your turn. One minute more is not going to change your life, unless you hurt someone trying to be a jerk; then you may have to stay for a while. It's not worth it.

Also, please make sure you have everything with you instead of jumping off your seat. People leave all types of personal belongings behind when deplaning: tablets, cellphones, laptops, books, magazines, and even their bags, simply because they cannot wait to exit the airplane. If you are traveling to an international destination or arriving at the US, getting those objects back may take a while, and you have only yourself to blame. Imagine trying to go through customs just to realize you left your passport onboard inside the seatback pocket. We told you to check your personal belongings before exiting the airplane, but your mind was already on the beach having a margarita.

CHAPTER 20

FREE AT LAST

This is the moment you have been waiting for - exiting that awful metal tube and finding your way out. I have to say I have had experiences on some first-class airlines that were so wonderful that I wished the flight would go on for a few more hours.

If you are connecting to another flight your first option is making sure where your next flight is leaving from and at what time. You can check from your phone or tablet using the airline's free app or just look for the first tv monitor near you. If you have plenty of time, find something to do or just wait around for your next flight. Depending on what airport you are in and the length of your layover I don't recommend exiting the checkpoint. I know you can't wait to have a cigarette, but it may cause you to miss your next flight. If you think it is worth the risk, then go ahead; you are an adult. If you have more than a three-hour layover and you want to go outside, you do not have to pick up your luggage, unless you are coming from an international destination to the United States. Then you won't have an option as described in the international chapter. For domestic connections, your airline will hopefully transfer your bags to your final destination, and then you don't have to worry about having to carry them outside. Make sure you have identification with you, as you may have to go through the checkpoint again. If you are traveling to another country it is always good to ask and make sure you have the visa or permit to exit that airport. I recommend in those cases to just follow the signs to the connecting gates, so you won't have to go through immigration and security again.

If you are arriving at your final destination, the first thing you should do when you come up the jet bridge is to look up and look for the exit or luggage pick up signs. Every airport is different. There are very small airports that will only take you couple of minutes to exit, and very large airports that will give you another wonderful tour before you find your checked luggage. Some airports are like small cities, and you have to pay very good attention to the signs. I remember getting lost at Atlanta Airport once. There was a point when I had no clue where I was, but I was also not paying very good attention to the signage. At some airports, you need to take a train or bus to the main terminal. That's when I'm glad I checked my bag all the way and I don't have to carry it all over the airport.

If you are coming in on business I hope you planned all your transportation needs ahead of time. If you company is taking care of everything, then all you have to do is to find your way out; the *right* way. All airports and terminals are set up differently. If you have a driver waiting for you, always call them as soon as you land so you can arrange the pickup place and time. If you are taking advantage of the many cities whose trains actually have a stop inside or near the terminals, you are one of the lucky ones. Cities like Chicago, Atlanta, Washington DC, San Francisco, New York, Toronto, Hong Kong and Beijing will offer those services if you are allergic to traffic. Remember; during peak hours locals will not appreciate you sitting inside of a train with five bags, taking up a lot of space.

I used to live in Boston. The last time I went there for pleasure I thought my Uber would pick me up at the same place as always. I even argued with the driver about the location until he mentioned the new pickup area. I had no clue that they recently created an area for those type of pickups. I felt horrible and gave him a very good tip afterwards. So, remember; always check for signs.

The moment you leave the airplane you should have an exit plan. Where, how and with whom are you going? Are you going to a hotel? Do they have transportation to and from the airport? Are you taking a taxi? You should already have an answer to that question. This way you know what sign to follow. Taxis may be in a different location than airport shuttles, etc. After the afternoon hours many airport arrivals get very busy as more flights start to land. If I take a flight to Fort Lauderdale Airport at night and my friends are picking me up, I always tell them to go to Departures. At that time Arrivals is usually extremely busy, and it will take longer to find a spot. Social media can be your best friend for getting information about a specific airport you are traveling to. There are always others who are more than happy to give you advice on how to get out faster, or about things to do inside.

Many people use car rental companies to transport them to their hotels, office, or other destination. Some airports, depending on their size, may have rental cars on property, while others may not. In any case, almost all airports with rental car services will have an information desk or board with a phone inside the terminals by baggage claim. Just look for the rental car signs. Always trust the signs.

Coming to Chicago O'Hare one time we had to wait for our hotel van. At this specific terminal there was a sign indicating where the pickup location was for hotel shuttles. It was a long walk, so when we saw some people getting picked up right across the road like at other airports, we decided to do the same, completely ignoring the signage. After waiting for over forty minutes, we decided to go inside and ask. We found out we were waiting in the wrong place. We were supposed to walk all the way to the left, take a passage under the road and come up to the van pick up location. Our driver was a little upset, and he was justified.

If you are traveling light or on a budget then the train would be your best option, as taxis can be a little expensive, depending on the city you are in. When I travel to Europe, I always try to use the same company. They give me a discount for my loyalty and I appreciate that. In comparison to a taxi, the price is almost the same, and sometimes it is much cheaper for better service, including waiting for me at baggage claim. I go comfortably, and I don't have to worry about carrying my bags on a train full of people, especially after a redeye.

If you are not sure how to get to your destination, always ask. Be very careful of people who will try to scam you and overcharge you for the ride - or even rob you. Always use the transportation approved by the airport or this can turn into a dangerous situation. Be safe. You can also take advantage of the free Wi-Fi many Airports have to offer and use the technology available to find your way out or your mode of transportation.

Traveling inside a large airport can be a little frustrating if you let it be. If they have a train to the terminals or baggage claim, take it. Why risk getting lost and not arriving at your next stop on time? The more stressed you are, the less likely you are to find what you are looking for. Relax and breathe. Thousands of other passengers have done what you are doing right now and survived. If I survived getting lost at Atlanta Airport, you can survive your ordeal.

Now, for those of you who have to pick up luggage before leaving the airport, it is very important to know what carousel number you are heading to. Some baggage claim areas are extremely large, and you may get confused, especially if you have no idea where to go. The TV monitors around the terminals will give you that information. Just look for arrival information for flights. On the right side it will tell you what the baggage claim number for your specific flight is. If there are no monitors, or if you just want to make sure you have the right information, ask a gate agent as soon as you exit the airplane. Just remember; some airports are faster than others. It is part of the experience.

One time I got home after a long vacation and I was tired. I checked all my bags because I was just not in the mood to carry anything with me, and I had some extra liquid inside. I arrived at the baggage claim and waited for my bags. After about five minutes, a gentleman started to get very anxious. His voice got a little louder and he started to make it clear he was really pissed off about the wait. I had been there about 8 minutes, and he got there right after me. Suddenly a local sheriff came and stood right behind him, just watching his actions. Then the bags started to come out. Another five minutes passed, and we were both still waiting for our luggage. He became really agitated and started to move other people's bags around, so the sheriff came up to him and tried to calm him down. I don't think he knew it was the sheriff, though, and he pushed back very aggressively. That was a big mistake. He came all that way just to get arrested at the baggage claim for being so stupid. My bags came out after only fifteen minutes of waiting. Getting upset or aggressive was not going to make my bags come up faster.

CHAPTER 21

CONCLUSION

We all like to travel. Some of us travel frequently, while others may do it once a year. Sometimes you even encounter people traveling for the first time. I call them Virgin Travelers. Now, travel can be stressful for everybody, whether they are frequent flyers or Virgin Travelers. In any case, I truly believe we are in control of removing some of the stress from it or adding to it. After all, we make our own decisions when we travel. We have choices. Nobody puts a gun to our heads to take a specific airline or to choose a time of day to fly. And if you know your airline will not give you any food, complaining about it won't change anything. Be prepared and bring your own.

I was doing a medium international flight in the morning on time, and even though we offered snacks for the whole cabin, we did not have hot breakfast. Every time I passed by, a lady decided to say: "Avianca has breakfast."

The first time she said it I apologized and informed her that although our airline did not have hot breakfast, she could have all of the available drinks and snacks she wanted. "I can't believe you don't serve breakfast; they do," she continued. After a while I started to ignore her as there was nothing else I could do or say to her. Clearly, she wanted breakfast.

About the fourth or fifth time I passed she said it again. Suddenly the passenger seated in the aisle across from her said, "Lady, stop it already. If you like them so much, what are you doing here? Aww, that's right; you saved four hundred dollars on your ticket." I wanted to laugh, but I didn't want to be disrespectful. She looked down and didn't open her mouth for the rest of the flight. I did thank the guy, and I just might have given him a cocktail on us.

So, you see; we create our own stress. She knew when she purchased the ticket that there was no food on board. She made the choice to fly on our airline. However, even if she hadn't known that, throwing a tantrum wasn't going to solve anything or make breakfast magically appear.

Another cause for stress for many passengers is when plans change. There are many reasons why a trip may not go according to plan, such as cancelations, delays due to weather or mechanical problems. It happens to the best of airlines. If you see there is bad weather at your departure city, arrival city, or in between, there is a possibility your flight may be delayed. Pilots can't take whatever path they want to. There is a flight plan - an invisible road in the air they have to follow. Just because it is not raining at your brother's house twenty miles away the airport it doesn't mean the weather is the same near the airport. I have even seen storms centered right above an airport, especially in Florida. Airlines are not trying to torture you or delay the flight on purpose. In fact, they may be losing thousands of dollars by doing so. Of course, some airlines are better than others at handling delays and cancelations, but communication is always the key. Getting upset or aggressive towards airline employees for any reason will not solve anything. Some of them may be as frustrated as well, as they have to deal with disruptive passengers and may get treated very badly by some of them. If you have any questions regarding your delayed flight, ask nicely. If you are afraid of missing a connection ask for help, but politely. Rudeness and aggressiveness will not take you anywhere. Sometimes it can even get you arrested. I understand the frustration but taking it out on an airline employee who isn't responsible for the delay in the first place won't help you at all.

Mechanical problems are another potential cause for stress. Just like your TV, car or boat may break, airplanes break, too, and they won't let us know when. It may happen suddenly. Would you get on a broken airplane if you knew? Of course not. Every time I fly for work or vacation and there is a mechanical problem, I am very happy they caught it before departure and someone can actually fix it. Let them take all the time they need. I want to be safe. It may take a little longer than planned but I will be happy to know there is no problem. People get upset every time a plane breaks, however, like it should never happen. How the airline manages this situation is key, of course, but still, there is nothing you can do at that point and stressing will only give you a stroke. The plane won't get fixed because you are mad about it. Making yourself a promise you will never fly that airline again doesn't mean you won't experience the same issue with other companies. I am sorry you experienced this issue but changing airlines won't stop that from happening again.

All the information you need for a pleasurable, stress-free trip is right there in front of you. There are signs everywhere, as well as social media and phone apps, and the best part is that most of this information is free. It's just there waiting for us to take it, and yet some still prefer the comfort of others telling them what to do or where to go. I often wonder how some people go through life asking before every single step they make. Don't be one of them. Go for it. Be brave. Be smart, and don't forget to pack your common sense with you.

THANK YOU

I hope you had as much fun reading this book as I did writing it for all of you, and also learned couple of things here and there. I wish you all safe travels and don't forget to be nice to others.

Boris Millan

Made in the USA
Middletown, DE
31 January 2019